And when he came to the place where the wild things are
they roared their terrible roars and gnashed their terrible teeth
and rolled their terrible eyes and showed their terrible claws
till Max said "BE STILL!"
and tamed them with the magic trick
of staring into all their yellow eyes without blinking.

Maurice Sendak
*Where the Wild Things Are*

# Seven Steps to Help Your Child Worry Less
# A Family Guide For Relieving Worries and Fears

Sam Goldstein, Ph.D.
Kristy S. Hagar, Ph.D.
Robert Brooks, Ph.D.

Foreword by
Edward Hallowell, M.D.

Illustrated by
Richard A. DiMatteo

Specialty Press, Inc.
Plantation, Florida

Copyright© 2002 Sam Goldstein, Ph.D., Kristy S. Hagar, Ph.D. and Robert Brooks, Ph.D.

ISBN 1-886941-46-7

**Library of Congress Cataloging-in-Publication Data**

Goldstein, Sam, 1952-
   Seven steps to help your child worry less : a family guide / Sam Goldstein, Kristy S. Hagar, Robert Brooks ; illustrated by Richard A. DiMatteo.
     p. cm.
   Includes bibliographical references and index.
   ISBN 1-886941-46-7 (alk. paper)
    1. Worry in children. 2. Fear in children. 3. Anxiety in children. 4. Child rearing. I. Hagar, Kristy S., 1966- II. Brooks, Robert B.  III. Title.

BF723.W67 .G65 2002
649'.6--dc21

                                2002075463

Cover design by Kall Graphics
Illustrations by Richard A. DiMatteo
Copyedited by Julia L. Parker

10 9 8 7 6 5 4 3 2 1

Printed in the United States of America

Specialty Press, Inc.
300 Northwest 70th Ave., Suite 102
Plantation, Florida 33317
(954) 792-8100 • (800) 233-9273
www.addwarehouse.com

# *Dedication*

*For Janet, Allyson, and Ryan*
*S.G.*

*For Chuck and Rachel*
*K.H.*

*With love to Marilyn, Rich and Cybèle, and Doug and Suzanne*
*R.B.*

*Thanks to Kathleen Gardner for her editorial support*
*and Harvey C. Parker for appreciating our ideas.*
*S.G.*
*K.H.*
*R.B.*

# FOREWORD

Worry is an alarm signal that goes off in our brains. When it sounds appropriately, it serves us well, but when it goes off when it shouldn't, it makes us miserable. It impedes our progress, leads to underachievement, and causes us to make mistakes. It can make us physically ill. I call this kind of worry "toxic worry," and it is a growing public health problem in the United States today. Toxic worry blights lives. It can infest your mind when you are just a child and can grow to monstrous proportions by the time you are an adult. Millions of otherwise healthy American adults suffer immense damage from chronic, toxic worry.

For most of human history people believed that the only "treatment" for toxic worry was to endure it, that it was simply part of the human condition, the price we humans had to pay for having an imagination. Indeed, the great 18th Century essayist and student of the mind, Samuel Johnson, called excessive worry "a disease of the imagination."

Now, however, as we are beginning to better understand how the brain works, we are devising effective remedies for dealing with toxic mental states, including depression, worry, mania and even psychosis. Indeed, one of the greatest achievements of the past fifty years has been the remarkable progress science has made both in understanding the biology of the mind and in offering safe and effective treatments for its toxic states.

One area of utmost concern is children. Unfortunately, toxic worry is common in children these days. For parents, teachers, and all others who care about children, it would be a godsend if we could have a reliable guide to help us help children learn to manage worry before it becomes toxic, keeping worry in the normal zone. Not only would this help children at a young age, but it would also dramatically reduce the likelihood of their suffering from severely disabling worry as adults. The sooner one learns positive mental habits, the more likely these will endure throughout life. The authors of this book have done a spectacular job in composing such a guide. It will help all who care about children help them deal with worry in such a way that it does not impair their lives now or when they become adults.

It is just as important that children learn to deal with worry and other toxic states of mind as it is that they learn to read or do math. It takes great expertise to teach these emotional skills; Goldstein, Hagar, and Brooks have succeeded brilliantly. As you read this book, and learn about the power of optimism, as well as its teachability, and you learn of the force of resilience, as well as its learnability, I hope you marvel, as I did, of the progress we are making, as a society, in child-rearing. Isn't it wonderful that we parents now have access to a book such as this one that enables us to address systematically and effectively a common emotional problem like toxic worry? For centuries, if a child worried excessively his "diagnosis" was that he was weak. And the "treatment" was to ridicule him in the hope that he would toughen up, or punish him, in the hope he would at least stay silent in his suffering.

Now, thank goodness, we can offer diagnoses based upon genetics and physiology, rather than on misleading ideas about moral fiber; and we can offer treatments that actually help, rather than make the sufferer feel and do worse. From that standpoint, it is a much better day to be a child—or an adult—than it ever has been.

As you read this book, not only do I hope you will learn and put into practice the superb techniques the authors offer, I also hope you will take pride in where we've come, and be glad that, at last, we are learning not to regard emotional pain as a sign of moral weakness.

Indeed, worriers—the audience this book addresses—are some of the bravest among us. They stare into a frightening furnace in their imaginations every day. They are also among the most creative and intelligent among us; after all, it takes a lot of creativity and intelligence to conjure up all those worries. But they need relief from unnecessary suffering, relief which this book beautifully provides. They can then take the mental energy they have freed up from worrying and put it into leading happier, more fulfilling lives. We have come a long way indeed.

Edward M. Hallowell, M.D.
Boston, Massachusetts
May 2002

# TABLE OF CONTENTS

# INTRODUCTION

## Seven Steps to Help Your Child Worry Less

# Introduction

# Seven Steps to Help Your Child Worry Less

### A Walk Down Bonneville Street

<u>The Gordon Family</u>

It is 8:00 p.m. one Monday night in November. The days have grown shorter and it is dark outside. Seven-year-old Michael is dawdling as he reluctantly gets ready for bed. Michael is afraid of the dark and of having bad dreams. Although he recognizes that there are no "monsters under his bed" or burglars in the house, he has a difficult time convincing himself of this fact. He cannot comfortably settle down to sleep. As a result, Michael resists bedtime and sleepovers. He has developed a variety of behaviors that often lead to conflict with his parents as he attempts to delay bedtime.

<u>The Barkley Family</u>

At the Barkley household next door, ten-year-old Susan is complaining to her mother that she feels ill and doesn't want to attend school the next day. Although Susan has not experienced problems with learning, attending school has always been difficult for her. Susan experienced stress when separating from her mother in kindergarten. In an attempt to ease her daughter's worries, Mrs. Barkley attended the first two weeks of kindergarten, sitting in the back of the room. However, Mrs. Barkley's attempts were futile, as separating each morning remained difficult for Susan throughout her kindergarten year. Although Susan currently attends school each day, she constantly worries that something bad might happen at home while she is gone. Her parents have grown weary of her complaints, and, in response, have encouraged her to "try harder" to not worry. For the most part, Susan has stopped telling them how she feels, but she experiences a pit in her stomach and a sense of nausea each morning when she leaves for school. She has tried to convince her parents to allow her to be home-schooled. Susan's parents recognize her struggles and worry that this problem may follow Susan into her middle school years.

## The Gardner Family

Down the street in the Gardner household, Kathy has just finished her homework. Kathy has always been very diligent about completing assignments, mostly enjoying larger projects such as writing reports and creating posters. Kathy enjoys school and is perceived by her teachers as a good student who is well-liked by her classmates. However, as the demands of school increase, Kathy's test scores in a number of subjects decline. Kathy's parents and teachers are perplexed by this change in her performance. They encourage her to take more time preparing for tests and worry that next year, in middle school, this behavior may cause serious problems for Kathy. Though they have attempted to understand this change in their daughter's functioning, Kathy has been anxious about telling her parents how she is feeling. She has developed a fear of failing tests, and now, just thinking about studying for a test evokes the same sense of apprehension that began to occur a few months ago as the teacher prepared to pass out a test. Kathy didn't understand that her worries about tests were now generalizing and affecting her in other areas of her life.

## The Cohen Family

The Cohens have three children. Each one's personality style is as different as night and day. Eight-year-old Melanie, with a sparkle in her eye and a bounce in her step, is the center of attention in social gatherings. Melanie is a "social butterfly," making friends everywhere she goes. Like Melanie, her 14-year-old brother, Alan, has never experienced social difficulties. He has a group of friends in the neighborhood and at school, many with whom he has maintained close, long-term relationships. In fact, just last year, Alan's best friend invited him to go on a vacation with his family. In contrast, 11-year-old Elaine stands apart from her siblings when it comes to social situations. She has always been rather shy and quiet. Teachers have repeatedly commented to her parents that they believe she is quite smart and would have a lot to contribute if only she would just make an effort to speak up. As a very young child, Elaine would hold back and hide behind her mother's leg when visitors came to the house or when she was out in public places. Elaine would really like to have more friends, but even the thought of approaching a group of girls on the playground makes her feel worried. Though she is not afraid the other children will reject her, she can't seem to bring herself to approach them or to speak up in class.

### The Ellefsen Family

Across the street, five-year-old Marty has just been sent to time-out. Marty has experienced some problems with his teeth and has been to the dentist a number of times. The last time, however, was particularly stressful and unfortunately painful for him. When Mrs. Ellefsen told her son he had an appointment with the dentist the next day, he told her he wouldn't go. When she told him he didn't have a choice he began screaming and crying. Mrs. Ellefsen sent him to his room. She understood that because the dentist visits were painful Marty didn't want to go. But she did not realize that Marty's fear of pain had been blown way out of proportion and he believed that he might die during his next visit. In an attempt to save his life, Marty was going to avoid that next trip to the dentist at all costs.

### The Neilson Family

One block over, nine- year-old Lisa, her two brothers, and her parents are planning on driving 300 miles to visit relatives for Thanksgiving. Lisa's family describes her as a "worry wart." As her brother, Jeffrey, puts it, "If there is something to worry about, Lisa will worry about it." Even though the trip is a number of weeks away, Lisa is already worried whether there will be enough gas stations, places to stop to go to the bathroom, and good weather. Though her parents have encouraged her to worry less, their advice has not seemed to make much difference. Even Lisa's friends notice her worries. Sometimes, however, Lisa is able to use her worry effectively to plan ahead. One time, Lisa and her friends decided to have a picnic in the park. In addition to bringing a blanket, Lisa decided to bring a plastic tarp, concerned that it might rain or the grass might be wet. Sure enough the sprinklers had just run in the park and Lisa and her friends were able to lay out the tarp and put their blanket on top. Lisa's friends thanked her for thinking ahead and bringing the tarp along.

## Worry: A Common Problem

As these examples illustrate, children differ a great deal in their worries and their ability to control those worries. For some children, like Lisa, worry seems to be an aspect of their temperament, while for others, like Marty, worry may develop through experience. While some children worry rarely, others find themselves caught up in excessive worry, unable to take actions to alleviate their negative feelings and resolve the sources of their stress.

Although worry comes in all shapes and sizes, every worry we examined on Bonneville Street had a common theme. That is, the inability to predict that whatever is coming up—bedtime, a test, recess, or a family trip—will turn out okay. In fact, simply put, worry results when we can't predict a positive outcome. When we can confidently predict what is coming, we are much less likely to worry. No matter the object of our worry, so long as we are confident and can convince ourselves that the outcome will be fine, we worry less.

Even in well-functioning families, under ideal circumstances, children worry. Parents are often unsure as to how to best respond, what words of encouragement to offer, or what strategies to set in place. Inadvertently, some parents may miss the source of their children's problems as stemming from worry or fear and instead respond as if their children are oppositional, resistant, or defiant. In these situations, parents often feel overwhelmed by the pressure to help. Thus, it is not surprising that the most common complaints parents have frequently relate to childhood worry.

For a child experiencing learning, behavioral, or other significant life stressors, a propensity to worry tends to fuel other problems. It is not uncommon for a child with a learning disability to worry about his or her capacity at school or his or her future. Ellen, an eight-year-old patient with a learning disability, explained that because of her school problems she was already worried as to whether or not she would have a good job and get married!

Most children, during their childhood, experience bouts of worry. Some seem to naturally develop skills to cope with their worry, while others struggle in silence. Worry left unchecked can often lead to anxiety and daily problems, leaving some children feeling overwhelmed or even frozen by their worry. Like worry, anxiety is one of the most common clinical conditions and reasons parents seek help for their children.

Our goal in writing this workbook is to help parents understand worry, fear, and anxiety in childhood. We wanted to show parents how they can help their child develop skills and strategies to effectively manage these problems. Throughout the book, we will offer positive practices and strategies that parents, teachers, and mental health professionals can use to help children master worry. Based on our combined years of research and experience with thousands of families, we have developed a practical, hands-on, seven step program to reduce childhood worry. As far as we are aware, this is the first program to address worry as a common problem for children. The chapters in this workbook represent the seven sequential steps necessary to help your child master worry, fear, and anxiety. Take a moment to review the seven steps.

# Seven Steps to Help Your Child Worry Less

## 1. Understand why children worry.

In the first step, we explain worry and the role worry plays in daily life. We will help you understand when worry and fear become anxiety. We will discuss the common worries of children and how they are affected by these worries. We will review the most common types of anxiety, including fears, separation, social, panic, and stress and we will talk about those children we call "worry warts." We will also briefly discuss the causes of worry, fear, and anxiety. With this step in place, you will be in a better position to interpret and understand your child's behavior.

## 2. When your child needs help.

In this step, we will offer a set of questions to help you identify your child's worries and to determine if they are interfering with everyday life. We will offer you a set of guidelines to determine when you need professional help. We will also provide an overview of the treatments medical and mental health professionals provide for anxious children. Finally, we will teach you a system to prioritize and define the worries you and your child have targeted to change.

## 3. Getting started—creating a working alliance with your child.

It would be wonderful if by simply explaining to your child the source of his or her problems and effective solutions, he or she would embrace your suggestions. Realistically, this is rarely the case. In this step, we will help you to destigmatize and demystify worry for your child. We will teach you how to help your child utilize a Worry Scale and a Worry Thermometer. We will provide you with strategies to teach your child about thoughts, feelings, and behaviors as well as the importance of thinking positively and having an optimistic mindset. We will offer suggestions to help you make these strategies part of every day life as well as how to change habits and negative scripts and how to teach by example.

### 4. Strategies to reduce anxiety.

We will offer step-by-step practical guidelines to implement effective strategies to reduce anxiety, including relaxation training, guided imagery, self-talk, debriefing, and desensitization.

### 5. Developing and putting your plan into action.

With an understanding of your child's patterns of worry, the alliance you have created to work on these worries, and an understanding of effective strategies, this step will help you develop and implement a plan to help your child worry less.

### 6. Common problems and how to solve them.

In this step we will identify common problems that often interfere with the success and effectiveness of your plan. Obstacles such as providing too much reassurance, making excuses for your child, being too directive, permitting avoidance, or becoming impatient will be discussed. Strategies will be offered to help you deal with each of these obstacles.

### 7. Instilling a resilient mindset in your child.

Resilient children are emotionally healthy and equipped to successfully confront challenges and bounce back from setbacks. Resilient children are hopeful and possess high self-worth.

They feel special and appreciated. They are capable of setting realistic goals and expectations for themselves. In this step, we will offer five key strategies to help you strengthen and foster a resilient mindset in your child. These qualities of resilience will play an important role in helping your child master worry and anxiety.

## Tips for Healthcare Professionals and Educators

There are two appendices. Appendix One is directed at mental health and medical professionals. It provides ideas and strategies to incorporate the use of this text as part of their treatment. It aims to help you understand how professionals can use this seven step program. Appendix Two provides strategies and suggestions for teachers. You may wish to provide this appendix to your child's teacher, particularly if problems with worry are interfering with school work, behavior, or social activities at school.

## Track Your Progress

Use this checklist to track your progress as you go through the seven steps.

— I understand why children experience fears and worry, when worry becomes anxiety, the types of worries children experience, and their causes.

— I know how to evaluate my child's worries and determine if my child and I require professional help.

— I recognize the importance of creating a working alliance with my child and have set in place a number of strategies to do so.

___ I understand the most effective strategies to help children worry less and reduce anxiety.

___ I have set a plan into place to help my child worry less.

___ In setting the plan into place, I have carefully searched for obstacles that reduce the effectiveness of my plan and have implemented strategies to deal with these obstacles.

___ I understand the importance of helping my child develop a resilient mindset and have implemented five strategies to do so.

## Summary

If you are concerned about your child's inability to master worry, fear, and anxiety, you are not alone. It is our hope that as you read this book, you will find solutions to these problems. The strategies and ideas you will read about are based on scientific research and practical experience. We are confident that following these seven steps will help your child worry less.

Our goal is to help your child manage worry effectively and thereby avoid excessive stress and the risk of developing serious problems with anxiety. However, if your child experiences significant anxiety, we believe that this book, as a component of a treatment plan directed by a mental health professional, can help you make a significant, positive impact on your child's everyday life.

# STEP 1

## Why Do Children Worry?

# Step 1

# Why Do Children Worry?

## What is Worry?

As noted in the previous chapter, children can worry about many things. Although the kids on Bonneville Street each had different worries, varying in intensity and evoking different reactions, they all had one thing in common—they experienced a sense of uneasiness or discomfort about something that could happen in the future. They worried because they were uncertain about what would happen, or they worried because they made a prediction about what was going to happen that had an adverse or less than favorable outcome. For example, Lisa worried about the family trip (uncertainty), Marty worried about the next time he went to the dentist (the visit might be deadly), and Kathy worried about failing tests (bad outcome).

### Why is worry important?

Worry can be considered a normal response to many situations. If children didn't worry (even slightly) about doing well—say, on a math test —then it is likely that they would not learn or perform as effectively. Mild worry can be a motivator to take action such as preparing for a speech, studying for a test, or training for a sports competition. A certain degree of worry also serves as protection and self-preservation. Children's worries about their own safety and the safety of their loved ones are common and can hopefully assist them in making choices that will keep them out of harm's way.

## What is Fear?

Worry associated with harm as the result of a specific animate (e.g., animal) or inanimate (e.g., airplane) object, leads to fear. Fear is often accompanied by physical symptoms, including changes in heartbeat, blood pressure, and hormones. In the extreme situation, this is referred to as a phobia. A phobia results in a specific, isolated, and persistent fear of a particular object, animal, or person. Fears become phobias when efforts to avoid the perceived fear significantly interfere with daily life.

Temporary fears are common in children—many being age- or time-specific. Some begin with a startle reaction to a certain event during infancy or toddler years, and, in some cases, progress to simple phobias. Many years ago, a psychology researcher, John Watson, attempted to develop a phobia in little Albert, a young child. He exposed the child to a white rat and simultaneously banged a pot with a metal spoon behind the child's head. The child was startled and cried. After only seven of these exposures, whenever the child saw the rat, he began to cry. Fortunately, Watson was also able to demonstrate that this process could be reversed by slowly exposing the child to the rat and bringing the rat closer and closer to the child. Eventually the child did not cry in the presence of the rat.

Mild fears are quite common in children of all ages. Girls, however, report more fears than boys. Children's fears appear to change as they mature. Preschoolers are usually fearful of menacing animals and the dark. Some even become fearful of harmless, fantasy characters. As children mature, these types of fears decrease and are replaced with more realistic fears involving social and school issues. In the adolescent years, teens may fear failure or criticism.

Researchers have identified five distinct groups of fears in children and teens. These are:

1. fear of failure and criticism from adults
2. fear of the unknown
3. fear of injury and small animals
4. fear of danger and death
5. medical fears

The ten most common fears reported in children include:

1. being struck by a car
2. not being able to breathe
3. a bombing attack
4. being burned in a fire
5. falling from a high place
6. a burglar breaking into the home
7. an earthquake
8. death
9. poor grades
10. snakes

Although mild fears are common in children, fears developing into phobias are less common. Severe phobias occur in less than 1% of children, while mild phobias have been reported to occur in between 5% and 7% of children. Animal phobias often start before age five, while social phobias tend to arise after puberty. Fears and phobias related to heights, darkness, or storms, for example, will have a variable age of onset.

## When Does Worry Become Anxiety?

Anxiety develops out of worry when, despite the efforts of parents (and even children themselves) to provide reassurance, the worry persists and grows. The anxiety then begins to cause significant problems. Children's behaviors change to avoid or minimize the triggers of anxiety (e.g., not studying for a test due to worry about failing, complaining of a stomachache every morning in an attempt to avoid school). While minor changes in routines are common and can be relatively uneventful (e.g., walking home from school "the long way" to avoid a scary dog), excessive changes in routines or behaviors to avoid anxiety-provoking stimuli are more troublesome and distressing (e.g., refusing to walk home from school at all due to unrealistic worry about being attacked by dogs). Changes in behavior can also be accompanied by physical symptoms of anxiety (e.g., queasiness, muscle tension, heart pounding). Worry and fear become anxiety when children cannot be reassured and their behavior significantly changes in order to reduce or avoid the feared object or situation.

How common is anxiety?

Worry and fear are common human experiences. Anxiety, too, is considered to be a natural and expected (though hopefully temporary) reaction to daily stressors, special occasions, deadlines, etc. Unfortunately, normal worry, fear, and anxiety have not been studied separately from clinical anxiety—anxiety that causes extreme distress and usually leads to seeking treatment. Therefore, it is unclear how many children experience moderate anxiety that falls between normal reactions and severely distressing and potentially incapacitating clinical anxiety. It is not uncommon for children to suffer in silence, and sometimes, only when parents notice a change in behavior does a child's worry, fear, or anxiety come to light.

How does anxiety affect people?

Anxiety can have a significant affect on people of all ages in various ways. Anxiety can affect the way we think about a situation, our behavior, and our physical reactions.

*Thoughts:* As we have discussed, the experience of anxiety involves certain thoughts, feelings, behaviors, and bodily responses. Thus far, this step has focused on the thoughts and feelings that fearful, worried, or anxious children develop. It is clear that they begin to think differently about their experiences, filtering what they see, hear, and feel in a negative manner.

. For example, while exiting a roller coaster, most children have interpreted the sensations of the coaster as pleasurable and enjoyable. However, others leave the ride and form an entirely different interpretation of it. They leave with negative thoughts and feelings—scared, concerned about their health and safety. Thinking about the ride as pleasurable is the furthest thing from their minds.

*Behavior:* Children develop a tendency to want to avoid situations that produce anxiety. In a previous example, a child starts to think about a frightening dog that he may encounter on the way home from school. He starts to worry because he can't predict for sure whether he will meet up with the dog that day. In order to stop the worrying, the boy decides to take another route home. His behavior changes in order to reduce his worry. While this can be a very adaptive problem-solving skill, it can sometimes lead to excessive avoidance (e.g., if the boy has to go four to five blocks out of his way) or an inflexible pattern of problem solving (e.g., if he believes he can never walk home that way again because he might see the dog). His initial avoidance of the situation, reinforced by the fact that he did not see the dog on the alternate route home, makes him more likely to repeat the same solution again in the future. This is called negative reinforcement. Negative reinforcement occurs when there is a change in behavior to stop or avoid an unpleasant, aversive, or unpredictable (the negative) feeling, thought, or action. The reinforcement part occurs because it feels good to avoid unpleasant things.

This behavior can be observed in everyone in certain situations. Avoiding unpleasant, uneasy, or unpredictable situations reduces anxiety. Unfortunately, sometimes children may also start to avoid situations that are similar to the original situation. In the previous example, a child starts to avoid walking home from school a certain route due to worry or anxiety about being attacked by dogs. Eventually, that worry may generalize to other situations (e.g., walking home from school altogether, to a friend's house, to the store, to the park).

*Physical:* Anxiety makes the body react—breathing becomes more shallow and/or more rapid, muscles tense, and the heart starts beating faster. While intense fear or anxiety causes the body to demonstrate noticeable levels of these physical signs (e.g., barely escaping danger in a car accident, giving a speech in front of 250 people), less intense anxiety-provoking situations can cause less noticeable and sometimes undetectable physical reactions. In any case, the body may react by clenching the teeth, slightly tensing the neck or shoulder muscles (a common cause of tension headaches), or developing a chronic shallow pattern of breathing.

## Types of Anxiety

In this section, we will discuss the different types of anxiety that can affect children. Phobias, separation anxiety, social anxiety, panic, stress-related anxiety, and generalized anxiety can each significantly impact a child's ability to function normally. Each type of anxiety will be described below.

### Phobias

A phobia is an intense fear of a specific object or situation that causes avoidance or extreme discomfort. Common childhood phobias include school, animals, heights, water, doctors, and loud noises. Children's phobic responses can be quite different from those of adults. While adults will often avoid or easily verbalize situations or things that they fear, children may have less opportunity to avoid phobic situations and may also have limited awareness and/or vocabulary to adequately express the things they fear. Common phobic reactions in children can include crying, tantrums, and/or clinginess to adults.

### Separation Anxiety

Separation anxiety is fear or excessive distress when separated (or separation is anticipated) from an important adult (usually parents) or place (e.g., home). Other symptoms of separation anxiety include persistent or excessive worry that harm will befall parents or other loved ones, fears of extended separation through malicious intent of others (e.g. being kidnapped), and not wanting to go to sleep without parents close by (also manifested by refusing to sleep away from home). Separation anxiety is an expected developmental phenomenon for children and is typically strongest during 14 to 18 months of age. As children get older, separation anxiety should significantly decrease. It is important to note that nearly all children, at some point, worry about their first sleepover away from home, their family's safety, or if they will be safe and not have bad dreams when they fall asleep. Again, it is when the anxiety becomes severe and persistent and negatively impacts the child's emotions and behavior that it is considered excessive.

## Social Anxiety

Concern about performing, interacting, or being embarrassed in social situations is probably one of the most common and normal worries that all humans experience at one time or another. How many times have parents worried about giving a presentation at work, hitting that perfect shot in front of golf buddies, or going to a party where they hardly know anyone? Common childhood social concerns include many of the same situations: giving a talk in front of the class, going to a birthday party, not wanting to strike out while playing stickball in gym class, etc. Performance anxiety becomes social anxiety when the fear or worry is persistent and leads to certain behaviors (e.g., crying, avoidance, isolation) when a child anticipates having to be in the situation.

## Panic

Panic or panic attacks can best be described as physical and/or emotional reactions to an anxiety-provoking situation or object. All of the types of situations described above can include panic attacks as a manifestation of the specific anxiety. Sometimes children and adults experience a sense of panic without a specific anxiety-pro-

voking stimulus. This reflects a strong biological component to panic. Children who experience panic attacks often provoke the most worrisome and concerned reactions from their parents, because their behavior can be so much more severe and demonstrable compared to other coping strategies such as avoidance or clinginess. The emergence of panic attacks often spearheads parents' motivation to seek treatment for their child's anxiety. Common physical symptoms of panic include tachycardia (heart racing), sweating, trembling, nausea, dizziness, hyperventilation, feeling cold or hot, numbness or tingling, and/or experiencing a smothering sensation. Emotional/cognitive symptoms can often include fear of dying, fear of losing control, derealization (feeling like things aren't real), depersonalization (feeling apart from one's self), having a desire to flee or escape from a particular event or setting, and/or feeling immobilized.

## Stress-related Anxiety

Stress-related anxiety typically occurs when someone (child or adult) has experienced or observed an event or series of events which are highly stressful or even traumatic. Consider the common example of test anxiety. It has been suggested that at least one-third of all students experience some degree of bothersome test anxiety. Suppose 12-year-old David had a particularly hard time on the last three math tests he had taken. As the semester progresses, like Kathy, David finds it more and more stressful to take and even prepare for a math test. While he may not necessarily avoid studying and may not be fearful of going to math class, his motivation, enjoyment, and perseverance in math is weighed down by the extreme distress he experiences just thinking about it. Stress-related anxiety can be paired with everyday, common occurrences that become aversive based on an individual's personal experience. In other words, while math class may be particularly stressful for David, many of his peers may enjoy the opportunity to learn math. There are, however, highly emotionally charged or traumatic situations in which most people would experience a stress-related anxiety reaction. Events in which serious injury or threat of injury occurs (either observed or experienced), combined with intense fear, horror, or helplessness is referred to as Posttraumatic Stress Disorder. Car accidents, violent crime, natural disasters, and abuse or other bodily harm are all examples of potentially serious, traumatizing situations. Children who experience severe traumatic events will be discussed in greater depth in step two.

### Generalized Anxiety ("Worry Warts")

Through experience, temperament, or a combination of both, some children are just prone to worry. These children tend to worry about all kinds of stuff, including many of the things listed above. When children's worrisome ways get out of control and excessive, either in intensity or scope, it is referred to as generalized anxiety. In other words, the anxiety they may experience in one or two situations generalizes to many other aspects of their lives. Like Lisa, these children often experience a "runaway train" of thoughts, feelings, and behaviors. They worry about the unpredictability of numerous events, situations, or activities. They experience a never-ending barrage of "what ifs" such as: "What if I fail?", "What if I don't wake up tomorrow?", "What if something happens to mom or dad?", "What if she calls on me to answer the question?", "What if that dog bites me?", and on and on.

## Causes of Worry, Fear, and Anxiety

### Experience

Believe it or not, a tendency to worry is much more common in some families than in others. However, this occurrence does not prove either an experiential, genetic, or environmental basis in the transmission of the problem from parent to child. As we have discussed, common sense tells us that many life events may lead to the experience of worry, fear, or anxiety. This pathway likely represents a number of factors, including the occurrence of the event, the individual's past experiences through which they filter the present anxiety provoking event, and possible genetic or biological risks that cause people to experience certain events more intensely.

### Genetics

As of this date, no specific gene or set of genes has been identified as responsible for worry, fear, or anxiety. At this writing, no adoption studies of anxiety disorders have been performed, either in children or adults. A number of twin studies have compared anxiety in identical and non-identical twins in an effort to separate genetic from environmental causes. Studies have focused on the amount of anxiety or fearfulness in the general population of twins compared to twins with significant anxiety. General fearfulness, particularly of the unknown, danger, or injury may be the result of a significant genetic effect. Panic disorder demonstrates the strongest genetic effect, while phobias demonstrate the weakest genetic effect. Additionally, of all the anxiety conditions, separation anxiety disorder may be more significant in females than males. What we do know is that when adults with anxiety problems are asked about their childhood, they often report multiple anxiety problems beginning at young ages. Perhaps by appropriately identifying those at risk for excessive worry and anxiety at young ages and providing them with the support, education, and coping strategies described in this manual, we may improve their lives.

## Neurobiology

Neurobiology refers to the structural and chemical operation of the brain. If there is a genetic component to worry, fear, and anxiety, exactly what is inherited? How does such a trait interact with the environment to produce an anxiety disorder or, for that matter, excessive worry. Researchers have not identified structural differences in the brains of people prone to anxiety. However, chemical differences have been reported. It appears that some children may possess a genetic risk to cause certain parts of the brain to either over-perform or under-perform. In very young children, this may be reflected as a shy or inhibited temperament. This shyness, however, may not progress into an anxiety disorder unless the child's genetic loading for this trait is unusually high or unless environmental factors combine with the trait to produce worry, fear, and anxiety. This fact provides the impetus for this book. That is, the more we learn about genetics, the more we realize that genetics may predispose some children to certain types of behavior, including worry and anxiety. However, experience may be the determining variable as to whether a child will learn to manage and cope with this vulnerability and thereby function well or whether the child will be overcome by it and exhibit excessive worry, fear, and anxiety.

## Summary

Worry and fear may be adaptive qualities, alerting each of us to the need to change or modify our behavior. These traits can become anxiety when they interfere with and impair every day functioning involving family, friends, and school. At the extreme, anxiety is a "whole body problem." It affects thoughts, feelings, behavior, and health. Although mental health professionals describe a number of different types of worry, all of these clinical conditions represent an uncertainty about what will happen and what can be made to happen. Though worry, fear, and anxiety are in part contributed to by genetic and biological risk, everyday experience combined with the behavior and reactions of adults ultimately determine the extent to which the majority of children experience worry, fear, and anxiety.

There are different types of anxiety. These include phobias, separation anxiety, social anxiety, stress-related anxiety, and generalized anxiety. In the coming chapters, we will discuss how to help children manage these different types of anxiety.

# STEP 2

## When Your Child Needs Help

# Step 2

# When Your Child Needs Help

Let's revisit Bonneville Street. Several of the families on Bonneville Street have children who experience some level of worry, fear, or anxiety. Bonneville Street can be considered a typical slice of life in many of today's neighborhoods, cities, and towns. The 21st century has arrived and, with it, comes increasing stressors, pressures, and demands. Fortunately, most children will endure these modern times with perseverance, resilience, and support. If worries and fears do arise, they are usually short-lived. Even some long-standing fears are not necessarily bothersome or disruptive to everyday life. For example, children who fear clowns will not typically rearrange their lives or restrict day-to-day activities to avoid being around clowns. They may not want to go to the circus, but in the grand scheme of life, that single avoidance will probably not prevent them from achieving their goals. The purpose of this chapter is to explore how worry and fear can develop into troublesome anxiety. We will help parents identify their child's worries and fears and determine if they interfere with ev-

eryday life. Lastly, we will explain when parents should seek professional help.

## When Do Worry and Fear Become Anxiety?

As we have said, worry, fear, and anxiety are normal human experiences. For most children, worries about specific things (e.g., anticipation about upcoming events or unpredictable outcomes) pass once they have persevered through the experience (e.g., doing well on a difficult math test). Fears, especially specific and developmentally normal ones (e.g., fear of the dark), usually diminish over time. However, when worry and fear persist, anxiety can develop, making a mountain out of a molehill, so to speak. Hopefully, even the more intense feelings of anxiety will be transitory and event or situation specific. Some children, however, seem more prone to worry, fear, and anxiety and have difficulty breaking the grip these feelings hold on them. Anxiety, in particular, can continue to rear its ugly head despite time, experience, and parental reassurance. Parents who have recognized that their child is worry-prone should determine the extent to which these problems interfere with daily functioning.

## Determining How Much Your Child's Anxiety Interferes with Everyday Life

Some forms of anxiety have only a minor impact on a child's daily life. For example, a child's fear of the night may affect his ability to fall asleep, but eventually he is able to sleep undisturbed through the night. Similarly, a child who is fearful of an object or situation to which he or she would not normally have daily contact (e.g., clowns or sharks) will probably not demonstrate a significant disruption in his or her functioning.

Other forms of anxiety can cause a child to suffer everyday and can significantly affect the quality of a youngster's life. For example, children with school phobia may not be able to separate from parents and attend school. Children with severe test anxiety, may not be able to concentrate effectively during exams and may be more likely to fail tests despite having the knowledge to pass.

Some children are particularly vulnerable to worrying and may become anxious about many different things, with little provocation. We'll call these children "worry warts." Sometimes exposure to everyday events will trigger a "snowballing effect" of anxious thoughts in such children. For example, just watching the evening news can be too overwhelming for them. A news story about the depleting ozone layer or a natural disaster may set off a chain reaction ultimately resulting in a child who becomes extremely anxious about safety and the safety of his or her family.

For some children, the demands of school, friends, and family can be hard to juggle. Even the activities that are supposed to be fun and interesting for a child can be stressful (e.g., finding the time to study for piano, getting to soccer practice, learning a difficult dance routine).

While it is unrealistic and probably impossible to shelter children from being exposed to distressing news events and the pressures of everyday life, parents should discuss and process these issues with their children. It is during this dialogue that parents can identify patterns of worrisome or anxious behavior that may require more attention.

The questions listed below can help parents determine types of worries their child may have and the degree to which such worries interfere with the child's everyday life.

1.  Does your child persistently talk about or seem preoccupied with a particular stressor or feared object/situation?

2.  Have your child's sleeping habits changed (e.g., nightmares more than once a week, avoidance of going to sleep, frequent nighttime waking, restless sleep)?

3.  Does your child avoid activities or situations he previously enjoyed (e.g., going to school, competing in sports, going to recreational or entertainment places)?

4.  Does your child complain of stomachaches or headaches (especially if the complaints consistently occur before a particular activity)?

5.  Does your child grind his teeth, especially at night (sometimes you can hear a

humming sound while your child sleeps, or ask your child's dentist about the signs)?

6. Does your child cry or seem easily bothered or irritated by little things?

7. Does your child seem jumpy, tense, or on pins and needles?

8. Does your child avoid sleepovers, especially when she previously enjoyed them?

9. Has your child's schoolwork or enthusiasm toward school declined?

10. Has your child reduced time with friends, or does she only want friends over at your house?

11. Has your child's appetite changed?

If you have answered positively to more than just a couple of these questions, worry may play a significant role in your child's everyday life. This is particularly so if you observe signs of anxiety which last for several weeks or more, if your child is unable to forget about or let go of worrisome thoughts, or if signs of anxiety affect daily functioning (e.g., refusal to go to school or to sleep).

## Seeking Professional Help

While our goal in this book is to help parents learn specific steps to enable their child to worry less, some children will need more help than their parents alone can provide. There may be times when consultation with a professional may be warranted. You might consider seeking professional help for your anxious or fearful child under the following circumstances:

1. your child's worry, fear, or anxiety increases despite you and your child's attempts at change

2. you or your child become increasingly frustrated when attempting to deal with these issues

3. you observe an extreme and sudden behavioral change in your child, such as severe temper tantrums, adamant or hysterical refusal to participate in activities, or withdrawal from friends and family

4. you observe significant changes in eating habits, sleeping habits (including recurring episodes of bed-wetting in an older child), and behavior patterns (these could be signs of a physical or emotional problem)

5. your child is exposed to a highly traumatic event (e.g., being harmed or injured, witnessing another being hurt, enduring a natural disaster) and experiences significant, unrelenting anxiety or change in behavior patterns as a result of such exposure.

Once parents conclude that professional help is needed, who should be contacted? A pediatrician or family doctor is often the first contact parents make. Consultation with a medical professional is a good choice, especially if children have physical complaints (e.g., stomachaches, severe headaches, tiredness). A physician can determine if a physical disorder is present and educate parents on the physical and behavioral or emotional changes that may accompany a medical condition. If a medical cause for a child's behavior has been ruled out, physicians may then refer parents and their children to counselors or psychologists.

Another source of information and help is your child's school. School psychologists and counselors are trained to help, especially if a child's worry, fear, or anxiety is school-related. School personnel are often familiar with other service providers in the area, both public and private, and can offer referrals to parents who seek assistance outside of the school setting.

When looking for someone to help your child, consider the points listed below.

1. Is the person licensed by the state in which they practice?

2. Have they been a counselor/therapist/psychologist for a substantial period of time?

3. Do they often see children or teens in their practice?

4. If necessary, are they willing to consult with your child's school?

5. Do they seem open and friendly?

6. Do they have adequate training to address your child's concerns and needs appropriately?

7. Do you feel at ease when at their office? Does your child seem to like them?

8. Do they return phone calls promptly?

9. Do they assess your child's needs and provide feedback to you, either verbally or through written reports?

10. Do they enlist your assistance in developing and implementing a treatment plan and a commitment to helping your child feel better?

If you answer "no" to any of the questions listed above, you should openly discuss those issues with the therapist. Any parent whose questions and concerns are not addressed or feels their child's therapist is unapproachable or dismissive should probably seek help somewhere else.

Keep in mind, however, that it is therapeutically appropriate for a counselor, therapist, psychiatrist, or psychologist to not discuss all of the information divulged by children within the context of the counseling session. It is important for therapists to maintain some degree of confidentiality with the children they serve. Parents who are uncomfortable or uneasy with that philosophy should relay their concerns. Children, and particularly teens, need to feel comfortable that the person with whom they are discussing their worries and concerns is not going to relay all of that information to their parents, teachers, or friends. The reasons for this are many and may include not wanting to be embarrassed, not wanting to worry parents, not wanting to get in trouble, or just wanting to maintain some privacy. However, therapists can effectively communicate with parents and solicit their support and participation without breaking confidentiality. They can also discuss with children and teens when they think sharing certain information with parents is necessary.

Once you and your child find a therapist with whom you are comfortable, you will all work together to address the child's worry, fear, and anxiety. While the methods used will vary from therapist to therapist, most will likely use a combination of behavioral strategies (behavior modification) and cognitive or mental strategies. Many of these techniques are described later in this workbook. Some therapists will have a prescribed number of sessions and an agenda for each session. Others may take a less structured approach and address events and/or concerns that are troublesome for the child at each session. Therapists will often assign "homework" which may include practicing breathing techniques or writing down a list of stress-relieving activities. Whatever method the therapist employs, parents should be active participants in helping their child follow through with the techniques taught in the therapist's office. Parents are often depended on to provide coaching and encouragement outside of the therapeutic setting.

The role of medication in treating anxiety.

Occasionally, physicians will determine that medication will assist in the child's care. This usually occurs when the child is demonstrating severe anxiety symptoms and/or when therapeutic intervention alone seems less effective. Medication can be particularly beneficial for children who are so anxious they have difficulty focusing on, learning, and applying the behavioral and cognitive strategies that can help reduce their distressing thoughts and feelings.

It should be noted, however, that for these conditions medication is best used as a short-term intervention and as an adjunct to cognitive and behavioral strategies. It is crucial for children to learn appropriate and lifelong coping skills to address anxious feelings and stressors as they arise. Current research suggests that learning these strategies is the most effective means of helping individuals cope with anxiety.

Nonetheless, as we have discussed, a tendency toward anxiety is a genetic or inherited trait that some children bring with them into the world. For this group of children, medications may not only be effective in reducing the severity of worry, fear, and anxiety, but they may be needed for long-term maintenance to avoid the resurgence of these problems.

Parents should be aware, however, that despite many studies demonstrating the effectiveness of anti-anxiety medications in adults, there are very few well-controlled studies of these medications with children and teens. This makes the recommendation about the precise indications for which children should begin drug therapy difficult. Further studies are clearly needed.

We suggest that you discuss possible benefits of medicine for your child if a trial of psychosocial intervention guided by a professional has failed or if your child's anxiety is so severe that he or she is unable to carry out activities of daily living such as attending school. The child or teen with severe separation anxiety disorder or panic attacks is a good example.

Two classes of medication, tricyclic antidepressants and the selective serotonin re-uptake inhibitors (SSRIs) have been demonstrated in research to be beneficial for children with anxiety problems, including obsessive-compulsive disorder. The tricyclic medications include imipramine (Tofranil®), desipramine (Norpramin®) and clomipramine. Among the SSRIs, fluoxetine (Prozac®) and sertraline (Zoloft®) have been researched particularly with obsessive-compulsive disorder and have been found to be effective. Although the benzodiazepine medications have been used extensively with adults, there is no strong evidence demonstrating the effectiveness of these medicines during the childhood or teen years.

## Deciding Upon a Plan

Once you and your child have determined that you want to address worry, fear, and anxiety, then you can start developing a strategy to move into action. In step five, we will show you how to set up and follow a plan to help your child worry less (the Worry-Less Plan). In developing this plan the family will first identify and define the worry to be the target of the plan. Next, different strategies to reduce worry will be identified and the plan will be implemented. While this may seem like an easy task for chldren with one specific worry, parents often find that what seems like an isolated worry is just a fragment of a larger worry or fear.

This can be illustrated in another household on Bonneville Street. Peter was an active and athletic ten-year-old. He enjoyed school, was a good student, and was well-liked by his peers. Early in his 5th grade year, Peter started to complain about going to school. This seemed out of character for Peter, who typically went off to school in the mornings with enthusiasm. Peter's parents recognized his increasing worry about school and quickly intervened. When attempting to identify and address the source of Peter's worry, both he and his parents thought that his dislike of school was just an adjustment period after a particularly enjoyable summer. Peter continued going to school with the encouragement and support of his parents. School eventually became tolerable, but not particularly enjoyable for him. Later in the school year, however, Peter began demonstrating a similar pattern of avoidance in regard to his piano lessons. With careful questioning and problem solving, Peter and his parents realized that his hesitancy and worry about attending school actually stemmed from greater worry about performing in front of people. Despite receiving much parental reassurance and the implementation of some coping strategies when attending school, Peter became overly worried and avoidant when anticipating his upcoming piano recital. While he was able to control his anxiety in one situation (classroom performance) the true underlying worry (performance anxiety) reared it's head when he was placed in a new situation that required performing in public.

This example illustrates how easy it is, despite the best intentions, to inaccurately identify worry targets, and jump into strategies that may not be effective in the long run. Step Five will provide greater detail and guidance on how to evaluate, identify, and address the most effective worry targets for your child. The information you get from considering the questions below can be used to begin this process.

## Targeting-the-Worry Questionnaire

1.   When did you first notice you were thinking worried thoughts?

2.   Can you remember what you first thought?

3.   Where were you when you noticed you were worried?

4.   What were you doing?

5.   What was different about the day/time/ situation that made you feel worried at that time?

6.  Was anything different, or did anything happen, the day, or several days, before you first noticed you were worrying?

7.  Are you worrying about something that will happen later or about something that has already happened?

8.  Are you worried about an experience or event that will be new to you?

9.  What does your day or week look like? Is anything coming up that is different, bothersome, or stressful?

10. Have you noticed if your body feels different (e.g., heart racing, feeling hot or cold, breathing too fast, holding your breath)?

You can help your child answer these questions and provide input about your own observations. For some children, the sources of worry, fear, or anxiety will be fairly easy to identify. For others, the sources of their distress may be less well-defined.

## Summary

The following steps will teach you specific strategies to train your child to handle stress and anxiety. It is important for everyone involved to be flexible in their plan as targets of worry may change and different strategies may need to be tried. If the source of worry, fear, or anxiety remains difficult to define or if an increasing pattern of distressed behavior is observed, the information in this chapter will assist parents in deciding when and how to seek professional assistance.

# STEP 3

**Getting Started—Helping Your Child
Become an Active Participant in the Process**

# Step 3

# Getting Started—Helping Your Child Become an Active Participant in the Process

One of the most important components of emotional well-being and resilience is the ability to distinguish between what we do and don't have control over in our life and to focus our energies on those areas that are within our power to change. When fear and anxiety become intense and prolonged, children typically feel increasingly distressed and overwhelmed. They struggle to gain a sense of control, but often their efforts lead them to rely on ways of coping that can actually intensify the problem. One very perceptive seven-year-old boy with separation anxiety said, "I'm scared to go to school so I want to stay home. When I stay home I feel better for a little while, but then I worry that I will never go to school and learn things."

## Nurturing an Optimistic Mindset: A Feeling of Control

If we want our children to deal successfully with their fear and anxiety, we must reinforce an optimistic mindset, a mindset characterized by realistic hope and a belief that problems are surmountable. A guiding principle in assisting our children to develop this mindset is to involve them as much as possible in the process of managing their fear and anxiety. The extent and nature of the involvement will vary from one child to the next depending upon such factors as the child's developmental and cognitive level and the intensity of the fear. However, even a small degree of participation will serve as a major force in helping children to become less frightened. Let's examine some of the things you can do as a parent to set in place and reinforce a feeling of optimism and control when your child worries.

## Be Empathic

A crucial first step is for parents to practice empathy. As much as possible, we must place ourselves in our children's shoes and see the world through their eyes. In the process of helping a child deal with fear and anxiety, empathic parents ask themselves several important questions, including:

1.  *"In anything I say or do with my child what do I hope to accomplish?"*
    In a situation that involves a child's fears, one of the main goals would be to help the child be less fearful.

2.  *"Am I saying or doing things in a way in which my child is most likely to listen to me and feel I really care?"* or *"Would I want anyone to behave or speak to me the way I am behaving or speaking to my child?"*
    In response to a child's worry, many well-meaning parents attempt to ameliorate the situation by saying, "There's nothing to be worried about," or "Try to stop thinking about monsters." Such statements, which are meant to reassure the child, fail to validate what the child is experiencing, leading children to feel even more vulnerable. If you were worried about some event would you find it helpful if a friend said, "There's nothing to worry about"?

3.  *"How would I want my children to describe my attempts to help them deal with their fears and anxieties and how would they actually describe me?"*
    If we want our children to work with us, they must feel we understand their distress and that we are their allies, not their critics. When they voice or demonstrate worries, we must convey to them how difficult it is to have worries, perhaps sharing a time when we were children burdened by fear or anxiety. If they experience us as empathic, they are more likely to join in the process of mastering their anxiety.

## Destigmatizing and Demystifying Worry and Anxiety

It is difficult to experience ongoing worry. The burden is intensified when this worry is accompanied by faulty beliefs that add to the child's sense of distress. For instance, some youngsters are concerned that their worry has made their parents unhappy or that they have disappointed their parents. Some are embarrassed and believe that there is something wrong with them for being so fearful; others think they are weak or crazy for being so fearful, while still others believe that they are all alone and no one else experiences the worries they do.

As parents, we must become as knowledgeable as we can about our children's worries and fears and then use this information with our children in a nonjudgmental, supportive manner. Since every child is different, if we are to demystify and destigmatize our children's fears, we should strive to learn their perception of their anxieties and correct any distortions they might have, especially those that are intensifying their distress. Thus, parents can convey to children that many youngsters worry about things, that some kids worry more than others, and that there are ways of handling these fears. It is important for children to feel that their parents will help them in a practical manner to lessen worries. It is also important for children to begin to feel that they are active participants in confronting their worries.

## Teaching Your Child about Thoughts, Feelings, and Behaviors

This section is closely related to the process of demystifying fear and anxiety for your child. It can be beneficial for your child to understand how our thoughts and feelings influence our behavior. Obviously, the explanation offered must be in keeping with your child's cognitive and developmental level. As an example, remember Kathy. Over time, she became very anxious when taking tests in school to the extent that the moment she came upon a question for which she did not know the answer, paralyzing fear set in and she could not proceed. She would just sit at her desk and not attempt to do any additional problems. She was not certain why she became so scared but did say, "I feel I'm so dumb. I think I'll never learn."

It was helpful for Kathy to learn that when she experienced these kinds of negative feelings and thoughts, it led to her behavior of just sitting at her desk not knowing what to do. Kathy's parents helped her figure out several things including what made her scared, what she thought about when she became frightened, and how she handled these feelings (i.e., her coping behaviors). Casting the issue in this way helped her to gain a handle on the problem. She realized that when she did not know an answer, she would look around the room, see everyone else working, and assume that they all knew the answers. This led her to believe that she was the dumbest kid in the class and that it wouldn't do any good to go further.

Her parents addressed the issue of feeling dumb and discussed that there were other kids who probably did not know all of the answers on the test. Her parents taught her ways to relax, especially by taking deep breaths. Finally, she arrived at what she thought would be the most helpful solution, at least in the short run. She requested to take the tests untimed and outside the classroom. While some students might feel singled out or different using such an approach, she wanted to test out what would happen if she were alone. In essence, she was actively reflecting upon how to change her feelings and consequent behaviors.

The intervention was successful. She felt less tense when she took tests without her classmates being present. When she felt anxious, she learned to sit back and take deep breaths and tell herself that she could proceed. Her test scores went up, and, within a relatively short time, her successes prompted her to take the tests in the classroom with her peers. Her confidence improved and her anxiety disappeared.

## Setting Up a Worry Scale and Worry Thermometer

When helping youngsters learn about feelings, thoughts, and behaviors and assisting them to deal more effectively with their worry and anxiety, it is often helpful to represent the frequency and intensity of these worries in a visual, concrete form. The very act of "concretizing" worry and anxiety seems to render these problems more manageable and less overpowering. One ten-year-old girl involved in creating a Worry Scale and Worry Thermometer said, "Now that I can see what's scaring me, it seems less scary." Such techniques increase a child's sense of empowerment and control.

A Worry Scale and Worry Thermometer can also provide children with a technique for monitoring and observing their progress and then making necessary changes in their intervention program. By using a Worry Scale and Worry Thermometer, children can gain a more long-term perspective of change. What follows is one possible form of a Worry Thermometer as well as suggestions of how to introduce the idea to your child.

You might explain to your child that one of the ways to see if worry and anxiety is becoming less troublesome is to measure the worry just as meteorologists measure temperature. You can list the two or three main worries confronting your child, and, under these worries, you can draw a thermometer with numbers from one to ten. You can say a ten is a very big worry, a worry that is very scary and one that you think about a lot. A one, on the other hand, is a very small worry. In this way, you set up a worry scale. Although some children may not know initially where to rank their worries, you can assist your child by listing something that causes him or her a great deal of anxiety (e.g., separation, fear of the dark) and something that does not (e.g., playing with a dog). The thermometer for the bigger fear can be at ten, while the little fear can be at one or two.

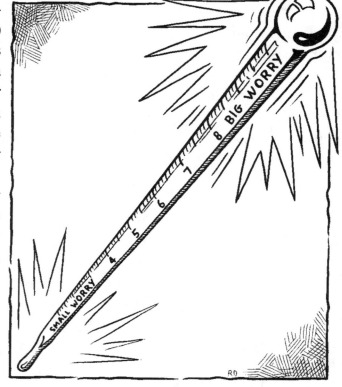

You can rate your child's progress on the thermometer every few days. This provides your child with a way to observe progress, to feel more hopeful, and to become a more active participant in the process of change.

## Developing
## Strategies with Your Child

An optimistic mindset is rooted in children believing that there are adults who can help them to help themselves. This is a critical belief, providing children with the courage to confront their worries and fears. We demystify problems and teach children about the links among feelings, thoughts, and behaviors. We can begin to change all three and create ways to represent and man-age fears and anxieties. Optimism is the best antidote for worry. To reinforce this optimistic mindset, we must engage our children in the process of problem solving.

In order to develop strategies to manage a problem, you and your child must agree that a problem exists. This typically is not difficult to accomplish when your child feels burdened by worries that cause distress. However, sometimes children minimize or deny worries. In such instances, parents must be empathic. Do not attempt to extract a confession from your son or daughter. For instance, if a child denies difficulties with separation but constantly experiences headaches or stomachaches when parents go out, the parents can say that many kids have some worries when a parent leaves, even for a short time. If the child denies that he feels this way, parents should not try to convince him he does. Instead, it's best to say, "Some kids feel this way and, if they do, there are ways of helping." Such a statement sets the tone to develop the kinds of strategies discussed in step four.

As Myrna Shure has highlighted through her "I Can Problem Solve Program" and her books, *Raising a Thinking Child and Raising a Thinking Preteen*, children as young as preschool age can be engaged in the process of problem solving. We can ask children to reflect upon several possible solutions to a problem and determine which one they think will work best. It is very impressive to observe the number of children who arrive at effective strategies, such as Kathy, who requested to take tests untimed outside the classroom.

Children struggling with worry and anxiety are more likely to have a pessimistic attitude towards interventions being successful. Parents can emphasize that if the first strategy that is selected doesn't work, then the child can try the second or third strategy. The message to our children should be that worry and anxiety are burdensome, there are solutions, some solutions may take time to be successful, some may not be effective at all, and, if that is the case, others will be attempted. We want to develop a realistic optimism and a sense of hope in our children.

## Changing Negative Scripts and Mindsets in Ourselves and Our Children

The process of considering and using new strategies to replace plans that have proved ineffective in the past demands that we, as parents, show the insight and courage to change our behaviors so that our children might change theirs. To use the same ineffective script repeatedly will guarantee continued frustration and anxiety.

Remember Michael, the seven-year-old boy on Bonneville Street who resisted bedtime due to his fear of the dark. When it was time for bed, Michael would find a million reasons to delay. When his parents attempted to direct him, he would eventually scream and yell, sometimes for hours. They viewed his behavior as oppositional and, out of frustration, they resorted to yelling at him.

But Michael was a frightened rather than an oppositional child. Michael's parents, with our assistance, asked him if he ever had "scary dreams." He looked surprised and said, "How did you know?" His parents answered that many children his age have nightmares. He seemed relieved to speak to us about these dreams, the main ones involving monsters pursuing him and his family. He added that he worried about these monsters under his bed. It is frequently helpful for young children to represent or concretize their fears, so we asked his parents to have him draw a picture of the monsters.

Michael drew the picture and mentioned that he was afraid to go to sleep because he would then have those bad dreams. Although Michael's parents had originally seen his bedtime behavior as manipulative and oppositional, they now understood it as a way of coping (i.e., an attempt to avoid the anxiety associated with nightmares). We discussed this alternative explanation of Michael's behavior, which elicited greater empathy on the part of his parents and prompted them to change their reactions.

Michael's parents also understood that their son could become an active participant in arriving at possible solutions to ease his anxiety and change his behavior. Much to their surprise, Michael offered two suggestions. The first was to have a night-light, which his parents had previously refused, believing that he was old enough not to need one. The second was truly creative, having a photo of his parents placed by his bed that he could look at when he became frightened. The parents agreed to both requests. Michael's tantrums and resistance to going to bed ended. His problem-solving skills, sense of control, and resilience were strengthened.

## Summary

It is not easy for parents to observe their children frightened and anxious. When this occurs, even well-meaning parents may fall into the negative script of telling their children what to do, of not involving them in the problem-solving process, and of becoming frustrated and angry when attempts to ease the anxieties are unsuccessful. If we remain empathic and remember that children will be less fearful and more willing to take appropriate risks when they sense our support and feel they have some control of the situation, then we can more effectively assist our children to overcome their fears. In the process, we also nurture their confidence and self-reliance.

# STEP 4

## Strategies to Reduce Anxiety

# Step 4

# Strategies to Reduce Anxiety

As mentioned earlier, worry, fear, and anxiety affect thoughts, feelings, behaviors, and bodily responses. In this step, we will offer step-by-step practical strategies to target and reduce worry, fear, or anxiety. These strategies include relaxation training, imagery, self-talk, debriefing, and desensitization. They are described below and can be used in isolation or in combination with each other. They often take practice, but with a little guidance and perseverance these skills can be used throughout your child's life (and yours too!) to combat worries, fears, and anxious feelings as they arise. You can explain to your child the rationale for these strategies.

First, we will focus on the bodily responses that worry, fear, or anxiety can produce and the strategies used to address these sensations. As noted in previous chapters, these feelings cause a physical reaction in our bodies. Imagine how you might feel if you just missed being in a car accident—your heart might pound, you might find yourself gripping the steering wheel tightly, and your breathing might become quick and shal-

low. Each of these reactions is a normal physiological response to stress. Read each of the anxiety-reduction strategies described in the sections that follow and determine which ones might best help your child cope with anxiety and stress.

## Breathing Techniques

Slow, paced breathing

One of the quickest ways to send a physical message for the body to calm down is to breathe slowly. This can easily be accomplished by modeling for your child and encouraging him or her to follow your lead and breathe at the same pace you are breathing. For younger children, one second in/one second out is a good place to start. For older children (ages eight or nine and up), two seconds in/two seconds out is suggested. (Note: these breathing rates are suggestions, but individual comfort levels with inhalation and exhalation will vary from child to child.) With more practice, your child will likely be able to comfortably extend inhalation/exhalation times.

## Deep breathing

This means breathing from the diaphragm rather than higher up in the lungs, which is called shallow breathing.  Again, this sends a physical message to your child's body to relax and calm down. It is important to learn to breathe from the diaphragm and do so in the slow, rhythmic pattern described above.  If the breathing is more shallow (i.e., the chest moves up and down while breathing more than the stomach), it could send the opposite signal and trigger the "fight or flight" response. At the very least, it will be a much less efficient way to get the body to calm down.

When initially teaching this technique to your child, it is helpful to identify how he breathes. Have your child place one hand on his chest and one hand on his stomach.  As he breathes normally, the hand on his stomach should rise on inhalation more than the hand on his chest. If the chest moves more, your child is more of a chest, or shallow, breather. It is often helpful to model this yourself. Adults are often good examples of chest breathers.  As we get older and deal with the daily stresses of life, it is not uncommon for many of us to gradually develop a more shallow breathing pattern. However, if you've ever watched a sleeping baby, you'll notice her stomach rises significantly higher on inhalation than her chest - this is how we were born to breathe! You may also recognize this technique if you've ever had vocal or singing training because you were probably taught to breathe from your diaphragm, rather than from higher in your chest.

## Airway technique

For optimal benefit of the deep, paced breathing, encourage your child to breathe in through his nose and out through his mouth. Breathing in through the nose moistens and warms the air going to your child's lungs, therefore preventing a dry throat or other discomfort. This too may take some practice.

## How to explain and encourage deep breathing to your child

For younger children (ages four or five to eight), the theme of the tummy being a balloon is frequently used. Have your child imagine the balloon filling up while inhaling and letting all the air out while exhaling. If your child is unsettled by imaging a balloon in his or her tummy, another suggestion is to imagine the belly button rising up and then sinking back in. It may take some creativity on the part of you and your child, but try to find an analogy or theme that your child can imagine and stick with it.

For older children, deep breathing can be easily explained and modeled with the sample described above (placing a hand on the stomach and chest, challenging/encouraging the child to raise the stomach more than the chest). Describing the "fight or flight" system of the body is also helpful for older children and adolescents. Explaining that worry, fear, and anxiety/panic are actual physiological responses, may provide a greater sense of control rather than children thinking, "It's all in my head."

## Troubleshooting breathing problems

*1. Complaining of feeling lightheaded when attempting deep breathing.*  Your child may be inhaling too deeply and/or holding his or her breath. Encourage and demonstrate relaxed, paced breathing. Correct deep breathing doesn't have to be a huge intake of air and should be just slightly louder than normal breathing. If your child seems to be holding his or her breath to model the breathing pace you've modeled or suggested, let him experiment and set a more comfortable pace.

*2. Stomach rises on exhalation rather than inhalation.* If this occurs, your child is using her stomach muscles to push out her tummy, rather than demonstrating the natural expansion of the diaphragm, which should occur on inhalation. Coach your child on the correct breathing technique. If possible, allow her to watch and listen to a baby sleeping. Babies are excellent models for the correct breathing technique.

## Relaxation

An excellent partner to deep breathing is learning to relax muscles in the body to achieve overall relaxation. This is often termed progressive relaxation, and the goal is to target individual muscles or groups of muscles one at a time, rather than trying to force the entire body to relax all at once. As with deep breathing, progressive relaxation takes time, practice, and concentration. Like learning to ride a bike, at first it takes a concerted effort to learn the technique. With each practice session, however, the body will become more and more efficient in reaching a state of relaxation.

Progressive relaxation consists of the child targeting various muscle groups and relaxing them one group at a time. Children can learn to take themselves through the relaxation technique, but initially it is helpful for parents to guide the relaxation efforts. As the child becomes more proficient, he may also enjoy making a tape of either his voice or his parent's voice, talking through the various muscle groups.

Suggested muscle groups include: facial muscles (forehead, cheeks, jaw), neck and shoulders, upper arms, lower arms, hands and fingers, back and stomach, upper legs, lower legs, and feet and toes.

Although personal preference may dictate the order of the progressive relaxation, it is often helpful, when first starting out, to begin with the facial muscles and gradually move down to the toes.

When first attempting progressive relaxation, it is often hard to determine how relaxed the muscles are. The tension/relaxation method helps to delineate the extreme difference between tense muscles and relaxed muscles and, therefore, may help children learn to relax their muscles more easily. The technique consists of focusing on a specific muscle or muscle group (e.g., facial muscles), tensing or squeezing the muscles for one to three seconds, and then attempting to totally relax them.

How to teach relaxation to your child

For younger children, it is often helpful to describe relaxation as being like a floppy doll or puppet. Modeling tension, using the analogy of a scarecrow or robot, and then demonstrating relaxation can be an excellent way to teach younger children. For older children (ages ten and above), describing relaxation as becoming soft as a pillow or cloud or "melting" into the cushions of a couch or bed are suggested. Of course, all children should be encouraged to come up with their own analogy or method of relaxing. It is also important to take into account the child's fears or worries when facilitating relaxation. For example, a child with a fear of heights probably would not relax trying to become "soft as a cloud."

If children have some difficulty getting relaxed, try this: when they get up in the morning, have them take note of how their body feels when they first wake up, before stretching or moving in their bed. This often helps give children an idea of how their bodies feel when they're re-laxed.

Troubleshooting relaxation problems

*1. Laughs when attempting relaxation.* Laughter is great medicine, and when the time is right, it should be encouraged. However, if it continuously interferes with the attempts at relaxation, state matter-of-factly that you'll help your child learn to relax later when he'll be more focused.

*2. Can't seem to focus.* Try relaxation later in the evening, but not right before bedtime, when your child has started to wind down.

*3. Can't seem to relax body parts.* Encourage your child to try to relax his whole body at once, rather than progressively.

*4. Can't find the right time to practice.* Try relaxation after a relaxing activity, such as a bath rather than after a high-stimulus activity like video games.

*5. Complains of not being able to relax.* Review the techniques your child is using and ask yourself the following questions:

(a) Is the analogy inappropriate or uncomfortable for your child (e.g., a young boy may not want to be "like a doll")? If so, try another.

(b) Is the environment distracting? (e.g., the family dog is barking, the television is too loud, other siblings are making noise or interrupting)? If so, find a quiet spot.

(c) Is the time of day inappropriate (e.g., all the neighborhood kids are outside playing and your child is inside trying to practice relaxation)? If so, change the time to practice.

(d) Are you a distraction? Does your child feel anxious having to perform in front of you or are you providing too much coaching or direction? If so, try to make relaxation practice more fun.

## Guided Imagery

Imagery is often used in conjunction with breathing and muscle relaxation to reduce feelings of worry, fear, or anxiety. Guided imagery is a technique often used not only for relaxation, but for goal-oriented performance enhancement. For example, many business seminars encourage their participants to imagine success on a presentation or project. Athletes are often encouraged to imagine their peak athletic prowess and successful crossing of the finish line to enhance their performance on the field. Imagery can often help reduce worry, fear, and anxiety by generating competing thoughts and images. For example, imagining yourself in a quiet, safe, soothing place often helps the body become more relaxed.

As with relaxation, guided imagery begins with a detailed, step-by-step procedure to help children imagine a certain scene or place. The themes can be endless, but common images include being on a soft cloud, lying under a rainbow, sitting on a beach, or lying on a blanket in a meadow. It is important to use an image or theme that is relaxing and not anxiety-provoking. For example, children or teens with allergies or asthma probably wouldn't become more relaxed imagining themselves in a meadow. Children should be encouraged to discover their own preferences, visualizing either real or make-believe places. It should be noted that imagining cold places (e.g., a ski resort, the top of a snowy mountain, etc.) is not recommended because it can result in more body tension, rather than relaxation. As with the other techniques we've discussed so far, it will initially take some time and extra effort to learn guided imagery. With guidance and practice, your child can master this very beneficial and enjoyable technique. Further in this chapter, there are two examples of guided imagery scripts. These scripts can be used or modified to create the most effective scene for your child. A helpful technique for some children and teens is to read, or have their parents read, the scripts into a tape recorder. The recording can then be used to guide the listener to his or her ideal relaxing place.

### How to explain guided imagery to children

Describing imagery and its benefits can be somewhat tricky.  In a sense, we are attempting to trick our body into thinking it is somewhere else, somewhere that is calm and relaxing, using only our minds. You may run into skepticism from your child, with them wondering "Can the way I think really change how my body is feeling?"  The answer is "Yes!"  Think of when you're scared or worried—your stomach might hurt, you get a headache, you feel sweaty or jittery.  These are body sensations that are caused by our thoughts.  So, you can fight fire with fire!

An excellent demonstration of how our thoughts and images can affect our body is the pickle trick. Have your child close his eyes and imagine seeing himself on his bed, the family couch, etc. Gradually and slowly talk him through the following phases, providing enough detail to help him imagine the scenes but not too much to lose his interest: getting up from the bed, walking down the hall to the kitchen, describe the kitchen and have him walk toward the refrigerator, open the refrigerator, and see a big jar of dill pickles; take the pickles out of the refrigerator and place them on the counter; then open the jar and take out the biggest pickle; lift it up to his mouth; and—take a big bite! Hopefully, your child will experience the sensation of biting into a pickle, even though he only imagined it.

### Examples of two guided imagery scripts

Read one of the sample scripts below to your child. Have your child sit or lie down in a comfortable place that is quiet and free of distractions. The larger of these scripts can be adjusted depending upon the age of your child or teen.

### Sample 1

Now I am going to sit back, relax, and close my eyes. Today I am going to go to a special place where I am as free and relaxed as possible. This place is secure and safe. My special place is a haven, a place where no one else has ever been. I want to go there now. I am in a forest of Aspen trees. I observe the beauty of the white bark against the bright autumn-changing leaves. The weather is cool, but not cold, and there is a slight breeze. The breeze rushes through the tops of the Aspens, causing some leaves to fall, the others making a wispy melody. I can hear this sound, and it relaxes me. It is a beautiful afternoon. The sun is shining brightly. The sky is a deep blue. The sun falls through the Aspens and forms a circle of sunlight on the plush green ground. I lay down in this circle. I am on a soft blanket. My hand brushes over it and I feel the softness on my palms and fingers. As I lay down I feel the sunlight on my face and hands. I feel bathed in peace and have a deep sense of comfort in my special place. I take a deep breath as I let the peace and softness of my special place spread through my entire body. I hear the sounds of the leaves and the drift of the clear, cool water of a nearby brook as it tumbles over the shiny, glistening rocks. With each breath, I become more deeply relaxed, with every muscle in my body becoming heavy, warm, and relaxed. I become more calm and secure with the peaceful and hypnotic sounds of the leaves whispering to me that I am safe and protected.

Sample 2

Now that I am relaxed and my body is free of muscle tension, I want to imagine my special place. It is a beautiful, warm day. The sun is shining brightly and there is a cool breeze. I am standing in a meadow of colorful wildflowers. Before me is a beautiful scene of nature. As I reach my special place, safe around the beautiful flowers, I sit down. I am proud and in awe of my view of the meadows and streams. I lean back against the single tree in the meadow—a large oak with protective limbs. The sun is able to make it's way through the leaves, and it falls on my face and shoulders. I feel this warmth all through my body. I am totally at peace. I feel the warmth of the sun as it radiates across my body and onto my shoulders. I feel the slight breeze in my hair while I hear the rustling of the leaves in the trees. My special place is calm and quiet. I am completely relaxed, taking in every sound and sight of the beautiful surroundings. My body feels no tension or stress, only relaxation. I feel the strength of the sun on my shoulders. My body takes in every soothing beam of warmth, further increasing the relaxation in my shoulders. I am completely at peace, and I am safe here in my special place.

Troubleshooting guided imagery if your child complains of not being able to imagine a scene

If you child has trouble picturing a scene in his mind, try some of the exercises listed below. These techniques can often help children become more confident with their ability to use imagery as a relaxation tool.

1. Encourage your child to imagine or try to visualize a dog, a friend, or a teacher and then ask questions (e.g., "When you are thinking of your dog, what is he doing? Is he sitting, standing, or lying down?," etc.)

2. Have your child imagine and describe a scene in his or her mind (e.g., a favorite playground, a landmark, an activity from the vacation last summer).

3. Have your child imagine the route from home to a favorite restaurant, school, or friend's house, describing all of the landmarks, traffic lights, etc. along the way.

## Positive Self-talk and Mental Distraction

In this section we will describe two thinking techniques to reduce worry, fear, or anxiety—positive self-talk and mental distraction. Positive self-talk consists of making statements to affirm feelings of control and to combat the negative self-talk (i.e., the "runaway train") that often exacerbates or perpetuates feelings of worry, fear, or anxiety. Mental distraction involves engaging in a mental task or exercise to compete against intrusive, negative thoughts.

## Positive self-talk

The way we think about a situation has a great impact on how we feel about it and how we react. For example, if I saw a snake and said to ourself, "I'm in trouble! I better get out of here fast," we would probably panic and run. But, if instead I said, "Stay calm. I'm safe," I would probably be more relaxed.

To use positive self-talk we must first look at the statements your child might be saying to himself that create fear or anxiety. Help your child identify negative thoughts he thinks when facing a fearful situation. For example, if your child is nervous about asking to join in a group, he might be thinking they don't want him to play or they don't like him.

It may take a little while to identify all the negative things your child could be thinking about a situation. Divide a paper into two columns—one headed "Negative Self-Talk" and the other headed "Positive Self-Talk." Make a list of the negaive statements your child thinks about when facing a fearful situation. In the second column, write some positive statements he could think about instead. There are three types of positive statements: affirming thoughts, relaxing thoughts, and realistic throughts that could be positive replacements.

Examples of affirming thoughts:
"I am okay."
"I am safe."
"I am strong."
"I am not afraid."
"I will try my best on the test tomorrow."

Examples of relaxing or pleasant thoughts:
"I am in such a warm and comfortable bed."
"I can't wait to see grandpa."
"I will get to make cookies when I get home."

Examples of realistic thoughts:
"Ghosts aren't real."
"That bad guy in the movie is just an actor."
"Mom and dad locked all the windows and doors."

Next, at the bottom of the paper, write this statement and fill in the blanks.

"Whenever I think (negative thought) _____ _____ I will stop and think (positive thought)_____ _____."

Teach your child to stop and think about his thoughts. This consists of teaching the child to identify the initial feelings or thoughts of worry, fear, and anxiety and then say or think "Stop!" Then, the child is encouraged to think of an affirming, relaxing, or rational thought.

Conquering fear and worry about a specific situation does not happen merely by replacing negative thoughts with positive ones. Parents will also need to spend time discussing the situation with their child and providing realistic reassurance. It may take time to build a child's confidence about a fearful situation. Your child may be skeptical even when told by you that there is no real basis for his fear. Showing your child how he could control his fearfulness by changing his thoughts, together with calm parental reassurance can be a great help.

### Mental distraction

Another method of reducing worry is to teach the child not to dwell on a worrisome thought and to use mental distraction. Mental distraction consists of thinking of a task that distracts the child and interrupts the negative thoughts or the "runaway train" that perpetuates or exacerbates worry, fear, or anxiety. As with positive self-talk, mental distraction works best when children employ it at the first sign of worry, fear, or anxiety. The themes for mental distraction can be endless, but some common techniques are described below.

#### Serial Sevens

This involves having the child think of a number and then subtracting seven from that number, then seven from that number, and so on. For older children, encourage them to start in the hundreds. Younger children can start around 50 and use their fingers if needed. This is a fun distraction for kids who like math, but for those who don't it might be more anxiety-provoking.

#### How-to's

This consists of having the child mentally talk through or mentally visualize through imagery how to do something (e.g., how to build a Lego fort, how to fix a skateboard, how to make pancakes, etc.).

#### Lists

Have the child think of lists for something (e.g., the ultimate trip to a candy store, what they want to take on vacation, what they want to do with grandma or grandpa).

## Debriefing

Most of us, at one time or another, have been greatly relieved by talking out problems, worries, or uncomfortable situations. Friends or family members who are ready to lend an ear and provide comfort, suggestions, and reassurance can help tremendously when we are distressed. In a sense, this is what debriefing is.

As most parents know, telling children, "It's okay, don't worry about it," or, for that matter to "try harder" is often insufficient to stop increasing feelings of worry, fear, or anxiety. Children who have the opportunity to discuss the things that bother them and are given accurate and realistic facts have the information and power they need to learn to confront negative thoughts and feelings.

The parents' role in debriefing is to help children identify, through guided questioning, the "what's," "why's," and "how's," that are causing distress. By engaging in this process of thinking out loud children can often gain insight about how to address and cope with their worries.

The following types of questions are samples of what can be used to begin the debriefing process:

1. When did you start worrying about that?
2. What happened that made you feel scared?
3. What was different that made you feel worried this time?
4. What was your first thought about that worry/fear?
5. How did your body feel?
6. Has that ever caused you harm before?
7. What makes you feel safe/strong?

Once children have started to discuss the "what's," "why's," and "how's," parents can provide specific information and reassurance that can be the basis for self-talk techniques. It should be emphasized that the process of debriefing is not to convince children or win an argument that there is no basis for their worries or fears. While parents can view debriefing as a fact-finding and fact-giving mission, it is important to provide empathy and not be dismissive of your child's distressed thoughts and feelings.

## Desensitization

The goal of desensitization is to face the situations that cause worry, fear, and anxiety in a stepwise, little-by-little fashion. The theory behind desensitization is that worry, fear, and anxiety are learned responses, often due to a negative experience with certain things or situations. Psychologists term this conditioning. The case of "Little Albert," described in an earlier chapter, provides an excellent example of how fear can be conditioned. Psychologist John Watson conditioned Albert to fear a white rat by loudly striking a metal pole every time Albert saw the rat. In Dr. Watson's experiment, Albert learned to fear an object (the rat, and subsequently other white, furry things) that would not typically induce worry, fear, or anxiety.

Parents can use the desenstization process to help their child overcome fearfulness associated with different situations. Start by identifying the situation (target fear) that frightens the child. Next make a list that is a hierarchy of situations that are related to the target fear (see the hierarchy about a fear of elevators on the next page).

When you develop this list of situations, keep the following points in mind:

1. It is often helpful to start with steps that involve just imagining being in a worrisome situation. This might elicit just a small amount of anxiety. Then add steps that cause increasing amounts of anxiety.
2. Each step should be a small step. It is important not to jump from a mildly fearful situation to a really scary one. Ten to twelve steps in the hierarchy is often a good rule of thumb.
3. Be specific. Write down in detail what each step will include.
4. Your final list can be altered as you go through the desensitization process. Revisions are encouraged to assure each step is reasonable and manageable.

After a list is composed, have your child practice relaxation and deep breathing. Once he or she feels comfortable, introduce the first step in the hierarchy. Your child might just imagine being in the worrisome situation. Encourage your child to continue to relax while thinking of (or actually being in) the worrisome situation. Explain that relaxing the body is "incompatible" with physical sensations of worry, fear, and anxiety. Therefore, this technique teaches the mind and body that there is really nothing to fear when in that situation. If your child can't seem to get relaxed when thinking of that first step, have him instead think of his safe place and congratulate him for his effort. Another attempt can be planned later, but encourage your child to try again soon if he seems to want to procrastinate. It is important to note, however, that working through the hierarchy is a gradual process. It is crucial to feel relaxed in one situation before moving on to the next. It may take only one or two attempts to conquer the uneasy feelings in each step of the hierarchy, or it may take 15 or 20. After your child is able to feel calm and relaxed with the first step, move onto the second, and so on. Don't rush through the list or be pressured to stick to a strict timetable.

Example: Uneasiness About Elevators

1. Imagine walking up to an elevator and standing in front of the door.
2. Imagine taking one step into the elevator and then step out.
3. Imagine stepping into the elevator and allowing the doors to close.
4. Imagine riding in the elevator.
5. Actually go to a building and stand in front of the elevator.
6. Take one step into the elevator and then step out.
7. Step into the elevator and allow the doors to close.
8. Ride one flight in the elevator.
9. Ride two to three flights in the elevator.
10. Ride four to six flights in the elevator.
11. Ride more than six flights in the elevator.

Troubleshooting desensitization

1. *The steps in the hierarchy don't seem to work, even the first step is too hard to overcome.* Try to rethink the hierarchy using the following guidelines:
   • If the first several steps aren't using imagery, then set up three or four imagined scenes as the first steps.
   • Perhaps the hierarchy is too specific. For example, instead of a specific discomfort about elevators, your child's worry may be more related to small spaces or heights. Ask more questions, and revise the hierarchy if needed.

2. *Your child says he's able to imagine being in an uncomfortable situation, but then complains he can't get relaxed.*
   • Reassess your child's relaxation techniques.
   • Review both deep breathing and progressive relaxation. If breathing, re-laxing, and imagining seem like too much to keep track of, encourage your child to try only deep breathing, while imagining the first few steps in the hierarchy. If that doesn't work very well, try the relaxation techniques instead. All children are different, and some may respond better to one technique than another.

## Summary

The effectiveness of strategies such as relaxation, desensitization, imagery, and positive self-talk reinforce our understanding of the power each human being holds to modify and guide his or her behavior. By incorporating these strategies into your Worry-Less Plan, you not only provide the means to help your child worry less, but you provide him or her with a lifetime supply of valuable skills.

# STEP 5

## Developing a Plan
## and Putting it Into Action

# Step 5

# Developing a Plan
# and Putting it Into Action

---

This step will help you develop and implement a plan to help your child worry less. We will call this a Worry-Less Plan. Your plan will include the following:

1. a list of things your child worries about, is fearful of, or is anxious about
2. times and places where these worries, fears, or anxieties occur most frequently
3. thoughts and feelings that your child may have that trigger the worry, fear, or anxiety
4. thoughts that your child can repeat to combat the worry, fear, or anxiety
5. activities your child can do to combat the worry, fear, or anxiety.

The Worry-Less Plan can be viewed as a contract between you and your child. Your role is to help provide guidance, support, and feedback to aid your child. You cannot make your child's worry, fear, or anxiety go away, but you can help empower him to learn to modify thoughts and physical reactions which, in turn, will give him a greater sense of control and mastery. Your child's role is to learn to identify and verbalize what causes him to worry. Your child must be a willing participant to battle these uncomfortable and sometimes downright scary feelings and situations.

Remember, children learn from observation. Part of your role in the contract is to model how to successfully cope with stress. Briefly take a look at your own coping skills. Try to think of how you've dealt with stressors at work or at home. Do you notice many of your child's behaviors in yourself? Do you always seem rushed, tense, or worried? If you are experiencing a high degree of worry or anxiety in your own life, it might be difficult to convince your child that things can be different. Remember, kids learn by example. Your approach to your child's worries and also to your own stressors should be with confidence that things can improve.

The first step is to figure out what your child worries about. Once you and your child have decided upon a worry target, then you can start a daily Worry-Less Plan. Soon we will ask you to make a chart like the one found later in this chapter to help your child keep track of his progress.

Take one worry at a time. It will be important for your child to determine when he feels in control of a worry before moving on to another target worry.

## Writing the Worry-Less Plan

You should start by writing a plan. To set up the Worry-Less Plan, you will have to answer five questions. You may want to refer to the answers to the Targeting-the-Worry Questionnaire you completed at the end of step two. Use the examples below as a guide to setting up your plan.

1.  What worry, fear, or anxiety does your child wish to improve?
    Ex. When riding in a car my child gets frightened we will crash.

2.  When or in what setting is the worry most distressing?
    Ex. The fear is greatest when we are riding in traffic or when it is raining and the roads are slippery.

3.  What specific thoughts and/or feelings trigger the worry?
    Ex. My child says he thinks, "I'm afraid we're going to crash!" or he worries, "What if we get into an accident?"

4.  What positive thought could your child say to himself to stop the worry thought or feeling listed above?
    Ex. My child could use positive self-talk statements such as, "Stop! Don't think about crashes! Everything will be fine."

5.  What activity could your child do to stop the worry thought or feeling listed above?
    Ex. 1. He could practice deep breathing

techniques to relax while riding in the car.
2. He could listen to the radio and keep his mind on the music.
3. He could bring a book in the car to read to take his mind off his worry.

Below are some examples of some typical distressing thoughts and behaviors and their corresponding worry-less thoughts and activities.

| Worry Thought | Worry-Less Thought |
|---|---|
| *I'm scared I'll fall.* | *I'll be fine if I hold onto the rail.* |
| *I'm afraid they will laugh at me.* | *They are my friends and they won't laugh.* |
| *What if I can't get out.* | *I've always been able to get out safely.* |
| *I'm worried mom might be hurt.* | *She is at work and she is safe.* |
| *What if I forget to do what I need to.* | *It will be okay, I'll just look at my notes.* |

Examples of statements describing distressing physical feelings or behaviors and worry-less behaviors include:

| Physical Feeling | Worry-Less Behavior |
|---|---|
| *Heart is beating fast* | *Take a few deep breaths* |
| *Palms are sweaty* | *Imagine a safe place* |
| *Body feels cold* | *Relax your muscles and imagine being warm* |
| *Hard to breathe* | *Practice deep breathing strategies* |

*Butterflies in belly*    *Practice deep breathing and think about something pleasant*

If your child is worried, fearful, or anxious about more than one thing, you might need to make up a separate Worry-Less Plan about each worry because there may be different thoughts and feelings that trigger the worry and different positive thoughts or activities that your child could do to combat the worry. It is good to start with just one plan and see how that works before going on to another.

For children who have mild to moderate fears, the Worry-Less Plan should work well. Using the strategies described in step four (breathing, relaxation, guided imagery, positive self-talk and mental distraction, debriefing, and desensitization) can greatly help reduce worry and fear. Combine body techniques, such as breathing and relaxation, with specific behavioral techniques and activities (such as a desensitization hierarchy). Consistently apply the methods written in the plan when worrisome thoughts and feelings arise.

Tracking progress

Use a chart to keep track of your child's progress. A good rule of thumb is to work the Worry-Less Plan for a specific worry for at least two weeks with ratings of only "1" or "2" for both frequency and intensity before you move on to a different worry. Don't be discouraged if your child continues to have some worries—all of us do throughout the course of the day. In fact, initially, there may be an increase in the degree of worry or the number of things that provoke worry. Try to reassure your child if he notices an increase in his worrying at first. It is normal to experience an initial increase in frequency or severity in any behavior we have targeted for change. All of the attempts to identify and find solutions for worry, fear, and anxiety raise our awareness of just how frequently these feelings can occur. It is important to stay focused and confident that things will get better.

## Making a Worry-Less Plan for Children Who are Worry Warts

For the child who fits the description of a worry wart, the list of worries, fears, or anxieties could be quite long. Children like this usually are anxious and worried much of the time and for a variety of reasons. For such children, it is probably ineffective to target specific worries and fears using the method described above. It is better to focus on *patterns* of thoughts and feelings that underlie their worrying.

When completing a Worry-Less Plan for this worry-prone child, try to identify a class of things that cause the child to worry. Does your child worry about his or her safety or the safety of others? Does your child tend to worry about the future and use statements such as, "What if (this or that) happens?"

1. What types of things does your child worry about?
   Ex. He worries about getting sick (catching a cold, throwing up, getting a headache) or getting hurt (falling from a bicycle, getting in a car crash, getting hit by a ball).

Next, try to identify the circumstances under which these worrisome thought patterns arise. For example, do they occur more frequently when your child is idle, tired, or bored? Do they begin or increase in anticipation of times of change or transition (e.g., a parent going on a trip, the beginning of the school year, etc.)?

2. When or in what settings is your child likely to worry most?
   Ex. He worries most when something stressful is coming up such as having a school project to do, going on a trip, or sleeping at someone's home.

3. What types of thoughts and/or feelings trigger the worry?
   Ex. 1. He thinks about how scared he is going to feel and starts getting nervous.
   2. He says to himself, "I can't do this."

Thus, for the worry-prone child it might be more important to target the negative pattern of thoughts which underlie the child's worries than the specific worry itself. Changing such thinking patterns can be difficult. The child should be encouraged to substitute positive thoughts for the worrisome thoughts they often have. They should be encouraged to use some of the strategies described in step four to actively reduce their focus on negative thoughts. Using positive self-talk and mental distraction can help. Thoughts like, "I am okay!", "I will be fine.", "Nothing will happen", etc. are examples of self-talk that can help the child reverse, instead of rehearse negative thinking. Sometimes the child will prefer to say one phrase over and over, or he may wish to recite a list of reasons why he should not worry. Mental distraction can also serve to take the child's mind off negative thinking. Getting the child to reverse, not rehearse negative thoughts can weaken the habit of negative thinking. As mentioned in step four, reciting lists, thinking about how to build something, recalling what you did yesterday, etc. are all ways a child can take his mind off negative thoughts.

## Making a Plan for Children with Obsessive-Compulsive Worry

Obsessive-compulsive worry usually involves a worrisome thought and a specific behavior that, after it is performed, typically relieves the worry. Unfortunately, this relief is usually only temporary, and soon the worrisome thought intrudes again, causing a similar need to perform a certain behavior or set of behaviors. The child cannot control the worrisome thoughts.

For example, a child may think, "Something bad will happen to my mother if I don't touch my bedroom door knob twenty-five times." The child touches the door knob twenty-five times and his worrying subsides. However, the obsessive thought comes back again and the child feels a need to react once more to reduce his anxiety.

Obsessive-compulsive worries can often quickly turn into uncontrollable and high speed "runaway trains" which can cause the child and his family tremendous stress. If your child demonstrates behaviors such as handwashing, showering, cleaning, counting, getting ready for school or getting ready for bed routines, or checking and rechecking that take up an unusual amount of time and are done repetitively or are performed in a particular fashion (especially if the child must start over if there is a disruption in the routine or ritual), then consultation with a professional is suggested. Managing obsessive-compulsive behavior is very difficult and will require time and expertise.

## Worry-Less Plan

Today is:_____
Anwer each question to form a worry-less plan.

1.  What worry, fear, or anxiety do you wish to work on?

    _____
    _____
    _____

2.  When or in what setting is the worry most distressing?

    _____
    _____
    _____
    _____

3.  What specific thoughts and/or feelings trigger the worry?

    _____
    _____
    _____
    _____

4.  What positive thought could be said to stop the worry thought or feeling listed above?

    _____
    _____
    _____
    _____

5.  What activity could be done to stop the worry thought or feeling listed above?

    _____
    _____
    _____
    _____

## Progress Chart

Today is:_____
Complete this chart each evening by circling one answer for each question.

1.  Target worry you and your child are working on to change.

    _____
    _____
    _____

2.  Today I experienced my target worry thought and/or feeling:
    1 = one time or less
    2 = two times
    3= three times
    4 = four times
    5 = five times or more

3.  How intense was my worry *before* I did my plan today?
    1 = not too bad
    2 = a little uncomfortable
    3 = bothersome
    4 = kind of intense
    5 = really uncomfortable

4.  How intense was my worry *after* I did my plan today?
    1 = not too bad
    2 = a little uncomfortable
    3 = bothersome
    4 = kind of intense
    5 = really uncomfortable

5.  Do I need to change anything in my plan?

    _____
    _____
    _____
    _____

## Enlisting Siblings' Participation

Solving a child's worry should be considered a family affair. While we have described your role and the role your child should play in attempting to reduce worry, fear, and anxiety, we now turn our attention to other family members who can play a supportive role. The most common supportive resource within the family, other than parents, is the child's siblings. With a little prep work on your part, siblings, both older and younger, can help foster a supportive and goal-oriented environment.

Perhaps the most important rule in enlisting siblings' help is to first let your worrisome child know that you would like to talk to his siblings about the worry-less plan. Don't be surprised if your child dislikes this idea. If your child insists that you not reveal his worries to his siblings then don't. Many children are concerned their worries will become ammunition for their siblings' taunting and, sometimes, rightfully so.

If your child agrees to sharing this information with siblings, there are a few things you should consider when doing so:
1. be as discreet as possible to protect your child's feelings
2. encourage your other children to be understanding and warn them not to tease or taunt the child with the worry
3. encourage siblings to understand the specific things they can do to help
4. if you observe a sibling being supportive, quietly show your approval.

When discussing worries with the child's siblings, encourage feedback about how they dealt with feelings of worry, fear, or anxiety in the past. While this may be helpful in relaying to your worrisome child that things can change, try to avoid comparing siblings' coping skills (e.g., "Lucy never worried about that when she was your age." or "Mike is younger than you and he doesn't worry about monsters under the bed anymore.").

For younger siblings, be less specific than you would with children over the age of seven or eight. Going into too much detail may cause younger siblings to develop the same or similar worries or fears.

## Addressing the Child's Worries with Others

Teachers

Other than parents and extended family members, teachers will probably be the adult with whom school-age children have the most contact. If a child's worry, fear, or anxiety occurs in the school setting or is solely present in the school setting, it will be important to enlist the teacher's help. Whenever possible, a child should know that his parents are going to discuss his worries with his teacher. Your decision of whether or not to enlist the teacher's help may depend on your child's reaction to others finding out about his or her worries. It might also depend on the grade your child is in and the circumstances that cause worry, fear, or anxiety in the school setting. For example, a child in kindergarten or first grade whose main worry is being away from home or her parents, will likely have a teacher who has dealt with this issue and can offer some helpful solutions. The teachers of junior high school or high school students may be more difficult to enlist because they tend to have many more students and a shorter period in the day when they can interact with and get to know their students. In addition, teenagers may be much more hesitant to have parents talk to teachers, as during this age they especially do not want to be seen as being different from their peers. If your child is hesitant to discuss his or her worries with the teacher, try to process this fear by asking questions about his or her specific concerns. It will be very important to discuss confidentiality with teachers and assure children that their worries will not be divulged to classmates. If a child is adamant about not discussing these issues with the teacher, it then becomes a judgment call on the part of the parents whether or not to disclose the information to the child's teacher. There are pros and cons to either decision. Telling the teacher may greatly benefit your child, but he may be angry or hurt if he finds out that you broke his confidence. Not telling the teacher may hinder your child's progress in overcoming his worry.

Regardless of the age of your child, you should obtain cooperation from teachers if you and your child decide to enlist their help. In many situations, teachers may only need to make minor changes in the way they deal with a worry-prone child. For example, for children and teens who worry excessively about being called on in class, teachers may decide not to call on them as frequently. Of course, the goal of this book is to help children overcome worry, fear, and anxiety. It is unrealistic to ask teachers to never call on your child, nor will it benefit your child in the long run to never experience situations to utilize the coping skills he or she will hopefully learn in this book. However, giving a child some temporary leeway while they work on these skills is a reasonable classroom adjustment. We know of one teacher who discussed the situation with the child and together they arrived at a solution, namely, the teacher privately informed the child

the day before what question she would ask the child in class the next day. Consequently, the child was prepared and less anxious in answering the question. As the child's anxiety decreased, so did the need for such preparation. Depending on the frequency and intensity of your child's worries or fears, involving the school counselor or the school psychologist might also be warranted.

Occasionally, a child's worries are so substantial that school performance is affected. In these instances, additional supports can be put into place to improve school functioning. For example, the school counselor may be able to provide suggestions and coaching of coping strategies specifically for the school environment. A child whose worries impact his or her ability to keep up academically or function successfully in the classroom may also qualify for accommodations under the Individuals with Disabilities Education Act (IDEA) or Section 504 of the Rehabilitation Act of 1973. The goal of these laws is not to exclude children from participation in school activities nor is it to absolve them completely from the expectations and requirements in the classroom. What these protections do provide is an assurance that children who may display significant worries and fears will not be discriminated against in the public school setting. Part of the benefit of these laws is a tangible, detailed document outlining everyone's role in dealing with a child whose worry, fear, or anxiety significantly disrupt his or her school performance. The documentation should outline strategies that teachers can implement in the classroom, as well as the expectations and participation of the student and his or her parents. Accommodations under these two laws are not written in stone. Once a child can function successfully, modifications to address school-related worries or fears can be discontinued.

If you choose to work with your child's teachers, we suggest you provide a copy of appendix two of this workbook, "Helping Children Worry Less at School: A Guide for Teachers" as part of your initial contact.

Coaches, scout leaders, community or church leaders, etc.

Depending on your child's involvement with extracurricular activities, there may be many other adults who interact with your child on a frequent basis. Several factors can help you and your child determine whether or not to enlist the help of other adults in the community. As a start, review the Targeting-the-Worry Questionnaire in step two. If distressing thoughts consistently occur in settings other than home or school, you may want to consider informing the adults in those settings. Discuss with your child his or her feelings about telling a coach, piano teacher, or Scout leader about distressing feelings and behaviors. Next, discuss and write a list of the pros and cons of relaying this information. If you and your child decide to inform other adults, discuss your concerns and wishes regarding confidentiality. Provide specific suggestions that may help your child and offer to brainstorm together to come up with potential strategies. If you and your child decide not to enlist the help of other adults in the community, it will be important to identify why you made this decision. If your child is involved with an adult who may not be understanding, or you feel he or she may be uncooperative, then a decision should be made as to whether or not to continue your child's involvement in that activity. If you and your child notice that there are several situations that cause distress, it will be important to reevaluate involvement in multiple voluntary or extracurricular activities. In some cases, the distress may be due to having to juggle multiple activities rather than the demands of the individual activities per se.

## Summary

This step has hopefully provided you and your child with a helpful model to identify, define, and prioritize the worries targeted for intervention and a framework to utilize the information, skills, and strategies obtained from the previous steps. Addressing a child's worry may require coordination between family members, friends, school, and the community. With all of these factors potentially involved, the Worry-Less Plan should be considered a work in progress that can be modified when needed. Problems and minor setbacks are not uncommon, so try to remain committed and provide encouragement to your child that positive changes can be made.

Step six will describe some common problems that may arise when implementing the plan, and step seven will provide information on how to instill a resilient mindset in your child when dealing with the potential uphill battles now and in the future.

# STEP 6

## Keeping the Plan in Place:
## Common Problems and How to Solve Them

# Step 6

# Keeping the Plan in Place:
# Common Problems and How to Solve Them

---

Once an intervention plan is developed and implemented, certain obstacles may arise that interfere with the effectiveness of the plan. The more aware we are of these possible roadblocks to success, the better prepared we will be to minimize or avoid them. Even well-intentioned parents may discover that they are not immune to facing these obstacles.

## Becoming Impatient—Remember, Progress Takes Time

All parents would like their child's fears and anxieties to be overcome as quickly as possible. It is painful to observe our children in distress. However, as we noted in step three, what appears to be a solid plan of action to alleviate fears and anxieties may prove to be markedly ineffective or may not result in a positive outcome as quickly as desired. If parents are not emotionally prepared for this possible occurrence, they can easily become frustrated with themselves or their child.

Elaine is a very timid, anxious eleven-year-old. As we described in the introduction, her anxiety was very noticeable in her relationships with others, especially with children her own age. She and her parents developed a plan to help with this social anxiety that involved Elaine saying hello to at least three of her classmates each day for two weeks. If she could accomplish this goal, she would move to the next goal and select one peer with whom she was most comfortable then invite that child to her house to play. Elaine succeeded at her first goal and at the beginning of the third week she asked a girl, Susan, to come to her house to play on the following day. Susan said she was busy and couldn't make it.

Elaine came home and began to cry and said, "No one wants to play with me." Her mother became caught up in Elaine's distress, and, rather than being empathic and engaging in problem solving, she said to Elaine, "You're too sensitive. If Susan can't come over, I'm sure there are other girls who can." While Elaine's mother's intent may have been to encourage Elaine to try again, Elaine experienced her mother's words as very critical, which intensified her sadness and anxiety.

When the initial plan was developed between Elaine and her parents, it would have been helpful to anticipate the possible obstacles or setbacks that might appear and to consider other options—back-up plans. These well-defined back-up plans tend to minimize the frustration of all the parties involved because you will know what to do next if a problem occurs.

It is important for parents and their children to establish realistic goals for progress and to view obstacles as positive learning experiences rather than frustrating and defeating ones.

## Too Much Reassurance

Parents may be vulnerable to offering too much reassurance in their quest to ease the worry and anxiety of their child. Offering reassurance is appropriate as long as it is realistic and does not minimize or invalidate a child's distress. However, when parents quickly attempt to reassure their children about fears and anxieties, children typically feel their parents are not listening to them or do not appreciate the emotional pain they are experiencing.

George, a seven-year-old, was a temperamentally anxious child. His parents remembered him startling easily as an infant and always "being fearful of his own shadow." He was fearful of noises in the house, frequently believing that a burglar was breaking in and that he and his family could be harmed. He was also fearful that a strong wind might knock down the large trees that surrounded their house, and that these trees would fall on to the house, causing extensive damage and possibly injuring a family member. After exterminators came to a neighbor's house to remove a beehive in the attic, George feared that the bees might find their way to his house. These fears were heightened when George was alone in his room, attempting to fall asleep.

His parents told George that he should call them from his room whenever he was scared. However, when George did so, his parents responded by saying there was nothing to be worried about, that the house had a good alarm system, that the trees were very sturdy, and that no bees had been spotted. On the surface, these parental comments seemed appropriate responses to lessen George's anxiety. However, in attempting to be reassuring, George's parents failed to validate his distress. They immediately told him that things would be fine without first empathizing with his emotional state.

It would be easier for George to feel comforted if his parents began with a statement such as, "We know how scary things can seem and how worried you are" or "We know that other kids worry about a burglar breaking in or something happening to their house." These words could then be followed by comments about what they have done (e.g., installing a burglar system, having the landscaper check on the trees).

While providing these comments and examples would not immediately end George's fears, they might provide the foundation or first step for easing his worries. To the anxious child, every fear is very real and not easily abated. Parents often must walk a tightrope, balancing the validation of a child's fears with a realistic appraisal and validation of those fears. The balance can be strengthened when the children are involved in a discussion of what would help them to cope with these fears, such as when Michael, the boy with the nightmares described in step three, suggested a night-light and a photo of his parents by his bed.

## Making Excuses and Permitting Avoidance

An obstacle that is frequently encountered is overprotecting our children in response to their anxieties, believing that they are falling apart and are incapable of handling the situation. As we noted earlier, strong, ongoing fear and anxiety typically does not just disappear on its own accord. If anything, parents and children must actively address and counter these fears lest they become more intense and debilitating.

Similar to the other obstacles, making excuses for our children or allowing them to avoid the situation, while borne out of love and concern, may actually serve to maintain the problem. If an intervention plan is not effective, the alternative is not to permit our children to run from the fear, but rather to face it equipped with a new and different strategy. When children resort to fleeing from their fears, they and their parents often learn a difficult, painful lesson, namely, that the fears are still alive, ready to emerge at any moment. The relief they have found in avoiding the situation is temporary at best.

If a child who is fearful of cats or dogs is invited to a friend's birthday party and the friend has a large dog, it is certainly understandable for the parents of the fearful child to talk with friend's parents about not having the dog roam the house. Most parents can empathize with the child's anxiety and keep the dog in a room or outdoors. However, even as these maneuvers are taking place, it would be important for the parents to figure out with the child ways for the child to become less fearful in the future.

We know of one girl who refused to go to her friend's party even when assured by the friend's parents that their two dogs would be kept on leashes outside. Rather than allowing their daughter not to attend the party, the parents worked out a plan that involved going to the friend's house with them the day before the party and seeing where the dogs would be. This was reassuring to the girl, and she was able to attend the party, although with some continued anxiety. The parents also provided assistance for her in the future, primarily involving her petting small dogs and slowly moving to larger ones. Although a temporary solution would have been to permit this girl to miss her friend's party and offer an excuse, they recognized that this would not solve the problem.

There are instances when a child is so overwhelmed with anxiety that any strategy is met with what appears to be a panic attack. In those instances, it may not be possible to have the child face, even in a toned down way, particular fears. Instead, professional help is strongly indicated. However, these are more extreme cases. In most instances, by using some of the strategies we have described in this book, we can help our children to learn ways to slowly manage anxiety.

## Being Too Directive

Fearful and anxious children require the assistance of parents who remain calm, strong, and protective. As we have seen, if we are not careful, protectiveness can slide into overprotectiveness, leading parents to become excessively reassuring or allowing their children to avoid the fearful event. A related obstacle, which almost represents the other side of the coin, is when parents become too directive, dictating what should be done without the input of the child.

Parents may be too directive both when planning strategies to deal with fears as well as when implementing these strategies. As we described in step three, it is important for parents to involve their children as active participants in the process of easing fears and anxieties. However, one can fall into the trap of telling children what to do, especially when we are stressed and frustrated. To be calm and firm in the face of our children's fears does not mean that we must tell them what to do. We must remember that a major component of resilience is a feeling of control over one's life, a feeling that is reinforced when we believe we have contributed to the solution to our problems.

If a child is extremely anxious, it may be appropriate, initially, for parents to suggest possible solutions as a way of highlighting that solutions do exist. Even in such a situation, parents would be wise to offer two or three possible solutions and then engage their child in a discussion of which feels most comfortable and which is most likely to succeed. The offering of choices can be done with any strategy we have discussed in this book, whether it involves relaxation techniques, guided imagery, desensitization, or other coping behaviors. When a child considers and makes a decision, parents can highlight the child's involvement by saying, "That sounds like a good choice. Let's try it and see what happens." Such comments reinforce a sense of ownership.

## Becoming Frustrated and Angry

Housed in many of these obstacles are our own frustrations and subsequent anger. It is very easy to become exasperated when our children demonstrate ongoing fears. When we are angry it is difficult to be empathic, supportive, or creative. Instead, parents might feel like screaming, "Stop worrying so much!", "Stop being such a baby!", or "Why don't you just try to do what you're afraid of?" Obviously, none of these comments will help the situation.

Since we are human, we can expect that, at times, negative feelings will emerge. However, just as we strive to teach our children more effective coping behaviors, we must have our own effective coping strategies accessible. Parents must discover the strategies that work best for them. We have known parents who have taken a deep breath and counted to ten and as they did asking themselves, "Is what I feel like saying going to help the situation?" Often the answer is "no" and thus, they don't say it. One mother observed, "When my son continues to say he is scared of the dark I want to scream, 'There's nothing to be afraid of,' but I realize that won't help. Instead, my new script is to say, 'I can see you're scared. We've got to figure out what will help.'"

Anger and frustration are much less likely to emerge if when planning an intervention, parents also consider back-up plans. As noted earlier, the presence of alternative strategies makes it easier to maintain a calm demeanor since it lessens our own feelings of hopelessness and helplessness.

## Not Knowing When More Is Needed

While we believe in perseverance and back-up plans, we also believe that parents should recognize when the original strategy and back-up strategies are ineffective. Each parent may have a different time table to measure effectiveness, in part determined by the level of the child's distress and the extent to which the fear or anxiety interferes with the child's daily functioning. However, a point may be reached in which parents have exhausted their resources. In such situations, professional help is often necessary, including a medication consultation.

One father poignantly told us that he should be able to find a way to comfort his child. We responded that being a loving, effective parent does not mean we can solve every one of our children's problems. Rather, it implies that we know when we need the support and input of a professional. If parents are uncertain if they have reached that point, they might wish to discuss the situation with the child's pediatrician.

## Summary

Being impatient, providing excessive reassurance, permitting avoidance, being too directive, and being short-tempered are all examples of the most frequent obstacles faced when achieving an effective plan of action. Roadblocks are to be expected in our journey to help our children deal with their fears and anxieties. The more we anticipate and recognize the possibility of these roadblocks and consider alternative paths to take, the better equipped we will be to find the best road to take in easing our children's distress.

# STEP 7

## Instilling a Resilient Mindset in Your Child

# Step 7

# Instilling a Resilient Mindset in Your Child

We all want our children to have success in school, satisfaction in their lives, meaningful friendships, and the opportunity to become functional members of their community. To realize these goals requires children to effectively negotiate the stresses of everyday life and deal with individual adversities such as worry and anxiety. Beyond our children mastering these individual differences, to realize the greater goals in life requires them to possess the inner strength to deal successfully day after day with the challenges and demands they face. This ability to cope, feel competent, and overcome problems is called resilience. Although we introduced the concept of resilience in step three, we believe this issue is so important as to deserve the final step in our program.

Resilient children are able to deal with stress and pressure. They bounce back from disappointments or adversity. They are capable of setting goals, solving problems, and acting responsibly. The skills that comprise a resilient mindset explain why some children overcome great obstacles, while others become victims of the stresses and challenges they encounter.

Regardless of ethical, cultural, religious, or scientific belief, possessing a resilient mindset is an essential quality, particularly for children prone to experience worry and anxiety. Possessing a resilient mindset equates to children carrying with them a set of tools to deal with whatever problems they face in everyday life. Children prone to anxiety and worry fare better when they become masters of resiliency. The concept of resilience defines a process of parenting that is essential to prepare all children for success in their lives. Each interaction with our children provides an opportunity to help them weave a strong and resilient personal fabric.

Resilient children possess a view of the world that enables them to meet challenges and pressures. They can translate this view into effective action. Resilient youngsters are hopeful and possess high self-worth. They feel special and appreciated. They have learned to set realistic goals and expectations for themselves. They are capable of problem solving and making good decisions. They view mistakes as challenges to confront rather than stresses to avoid. They have developed the interpersonal skills to deal successfully with peers and adults. These qualities, however, are not acquired from a pill or class. They are provided by parents possessing a mindset to foster resilience in their children. Parents possessing this mindset are guided by a blueprint of important principles, ideas, and actions. In step seven, we will define strategies and guidelines to help your children develop five important resilience qualities. We will introduce each quality and then offer some strategies and suggestions to consider in your day-in and day-out parenting. We believe that by providing children at risk for worry, fear, and anxiety with these strategies, we strengthen their resolve and their ability to utilize and benefit from the skills we provide to help them worry less.

## Feeling Special and Appreciated

When children feel loved and accepted, they also feel special and appreciated in the eyes of others. They believe they hold a special place in the hearts and minds of their parents. They sense that their parents enjoy being with them and know that their parents appreciate them. In this way, parents can act as "charismatic adults" in the lives of their children. The late psychologist, Dr. Julius Segal, coined this term to describe adults who, in their interactions with children, convey love, acceptance, and support—all qualities that help children feel special and appreciated. From such adults, children gather strength. This foundation is critically important to instill in children the courage to face their worry, fear, and anxiety. Feeling loved, special, and appreciated is a cornerstone of helping children develop a resilient mindset. It is little wonder that adults who

have overcome great childhood adversity often attribute their success to at least one adult who was there for them in trying times during childhood and adolescent years.

Every interaction with your children is an opportunity to engage in a process of helping them feel loved, special, and appreciated. Granted, in some situations, this is more difficult to accomplish, but those are the very situations in which it is vital to reinforce a resilient mindset. Following are six strategies to help you in this process:

1. *Let your memories of childhood be your guide*. We must incorporate into our parenting practices those experiences that helped us feel loved as well as those that did not. We should strive to avoid saying or doing things that led us to feel less worthy and less loved as children and, in many cases, as adults.

2. *Create traditions and special times.* Creating traditions and time set aside each day, week, or month as special with your children establishes an atmosphere in which they feel loved and appreciated. In doing so we convey the message to them that they are important to us and we enjoy being with them.

3. *Don't miss significant occasions.* If we are not present for the important events in our children's lives, they are likely to feel unimportant. Time, particularly during special events, invested in our children pays future dividends in the time they will invest in us as adults, allowing us to share in their adult lives as well.

4. *Be demonstrative with your love.* Although some parents find it difficult to display affection, we must all strive to let our children know they are loved on a daily basis.

5. *Build up, don't chip away at your children.* As parents we routinely engage in a chipping process without realizing it. We pronounce what our children are doing wrong rather than what they are doing right. We correct rather than teach. In doing so, we erode, or fail to reinforce, the features of a resilient mindset. It is difficult to develop a sense of self-worth, security, and confidence in the presence of people who are unappreciative.

6. *Accept your children.* A major theme of this workbook is accepting children for who they are and helping them overcome the adversities they face. The best way to help children change self-defeating behaviors is to create an atmosphere in which they feel safe and secure. In such a climate, they are able to recognize that what we are attempting to teach them is based firmly on our unconditional love. We expand on this point as a separate section below.

## Accepting Our Children for Who They Are

Nurturing a resilient mindset requires unconditional love and acceptance of our children. Keep in mind that fairness and acceptance are not synonymous with treating each child the same or having the same expectations and goals for each child. Fairness is demonstrated by responding to each child based on the child's particular temperament and needs. This type of acceptance is a foundation of resilience. As we have noted, acceptance is rooted in unconditional love and provides an environment for the reinforcement of a resilient mindset. When children feel accepted, they are more likely to be secure and confident, particularly in facing challenges and adversities. A basic premise of this workbook is the acceptance by parents that some children temperamentally come into the world more likely to experience daily events such as worry, fear, or anxiety. As children grow, this difference is manifested in the ways they learn, the activities in which they engage, and their ease in dealing with daily life. We must avoid falling into the trap of telling our children we accept them, but... (e.g., "We love you when you get good grades or clean your room."). Acceptance must serve as the link between our love and the process of defining realistic and obtainable goals with our children. Following are five strategies to help in the acceptance process:

1. *Become educated.* The key to your effort is to become familiar with your child's temperament, development, and behavior and use this information pro-actively in planning parenting practices. By understanding and accepting the unique qualities of each child we can best assist in fostering a resilient mindset.

2. *Measure your mindset.* Honestly consider your reactions in the past to your child's worrisome, fearful, or anxious behavior. In step three, we discussed the importance of empathy

in helping children begin to deal with their problems. Make certain that you always begin with empathy.

3. *Make necessary adjustments.* If there is a good match between your expectations and what your children can do, you stand the best chance of helping them overcome worry and anxiety. We don't suggest you give up your dreams and wishes, but realistically understand where your children are at, and help them work forward from that point. Thus, we suggest you separate your dreams for your children from who they are as individuals. Be careful to not impose expectations upon them based on your needs, interests, or goals.

4. *Begin the process of collaboration.* The basis of this book is collaboration between you and your children. Once you learn to accept your children for who they are, gain a clearer picture of each child's temperament and style, and begin to make changes in your behavior, it is easier for you to engage them in problem-solving discussions of appropriate goals and expectations. When we convey expectations in an accepting,

loving, and supportive manner, our children feel motivated to exceed those expectations.

## Nurturing Islands of Competence

One of the authors, Dr. Robert Brooks, coined the term "islands of competence" to describe activities that children engage in successfully and during which they experience enhanced self-confidence and self-esteem. In their book, *Raising Resilient Children* (Contemporary Books/ McGraw-Hill, 2001), Drs. Brooks and Goldstein point out that a celebratory process day-in and day-out helps children to develop skill and competence and nurtures a strong, resilient mindset. These experiences nurture a sense of mastery and capability and equip us to face new challenges and adversities. By helping your child develop an island of competence regardless of the skill, area, or ability involved, you strengthen your child's confidence to confront and overcome worry, fear, and anxiety. In doing so, we must avoid defining success for our children, but rather assist them in developing their own definitions. We must avoid setting the bar too high for them or unintentionally reinforcing low self-esteem when, after repeated trials, they may continue to be unsuccessful. Following are five strategies to help your children experience success and to nurture islands of competence:

1. *Openly enjoy and celebrate your children's accomplishments.* As our children grow they encounter countless challenges. Although these may seem like small steps to us, to your children they represent major advances. Each mastery brings with it a sense of success and accomplishment. Each mastery strengthens a child's resolve to deal with new challenges such as worry or anxiety. Children will feel more successful and supported when their achievements are acknowledged and appreciated.

2. *Emphasize your children's input in creating success.* Children capable of accepting ownership for their successes will develop high self-esteem. Your guiding principle must be to provide experiences and offer comments that convey to your children that they are active participants in what transpires in their lives. This is particularly important in shaping your child's mindset and perception of his or her capability to overcome worry, fear, and anxiety. In doing so, we perform a balancing act, namely, being available to assist our children, but not doing everything for them.

3. *Identify and reinforce your child's islands of competence.* It is important for you to identify and reinforce these islands and appreciate that they may differ from one child to the next. If

we want children experiencing worry, fear, and anxiety to overcome a defeatist mindset, we must help them develop self-worth and self-confidence through successful experiences. Remember also that children will feel greater ownership for their success when they experience these as meaningful to their lives.

4. *Give strengths time to develop.* Many children require time to develop and mature. If your child demonstrates an interest in a particular activity, even if his or her skills are below average compared to others, we must, within reason, support and nurture the development of these skills. We can never be certain which skills will someday become a child's islands of competence, reinforcing a sense of success, and, most important, a resilient mindset.

5. *Accept the unique strengths and successes of each child.* Children are aware of our disappointments when they don't meet our expectations and are particularly sensitive when their successes are not viewed as important or relevant by parents. We must, through our words and actions, communicate to our children that we accept them and believe in their capabilities. It is impossible to conceive of children developing a resilient mindset or, for that matter, overcoming worry and anxiety if they do not experience the joy and excitement of success in areas that they and significant others in their lives deem to be important.

## Learning from Mistakes

The ways in which a child understands and responds to mistakes is an integral feature of a resilient mindset. Some children are motivated by mistakes to succeed, while others appear defeated. Children often develop a negative view of mistakes. They frequently resort to counterproductive coping strategies such as avoidance, denial, or simply feeling inadequate in dealing with their perceived failure. Some children are at risk to develop this pattern biologically—that is, they appear to come to the world more likely to interpret mistakes as a sign of inadequacy. However, the negative comments of parents, excessive expectations, and the sense of learned helplessness some children develop when they struggle repeatedly are all obstacles in the process of helping children learn to deal effectively with mistakes. By helping children view mistakes as temporary setbacks and opportunities for learning rather than as indictments of their abilities, we assist them in developing a resilient mindset. Following are five strategies that you can use to help your children become comfortable with the role mistakes play in life:

1. *Serve as a model for dealing with mistakes and setbacks.* We are the primary models for our children. Our words and actions in response to life's daily challenges affect our children. If children witness parents backing away from challenges and quitting at tasks, they shouldn't be surprised when their children follow the same course of action. Children may not always do what we say, but they often do what we do.

2. *Set and evaluate realistic expectations.* In our well-meant efforts to help our children, we often set the bar too high. By expecting more from children than they are capable of giving, we rob them of the opportunity of learning to view mistakes as challenges. Instead, we create a climate in which children retreat from mistakes. The very fact that you have purchased and read this book means that you recognize the need to accept your child's current ability to deal with worry, fear, or anxiety as a basis for helping him or her develop mastery over these problems.

3. *In different ways, emphasize that mistakes are not only accepted but also expected.* We must communicate that mistakes are a natural part of life. It is important to develop a positive, less defeatist attitude toward mistakes. You can serve as a model. If you spill something or if you forget something, attempt to remain calm, verbalize what you could do to lessen the probability of making the same mistake again, and, when possible, use humor.

4. *Your love should not be contingent on whether or not your children make mistakes.* Many children believe they are accepted and loved only when they do not make mistakes and when they do not fail. Often this belief is intensified when parents hold expectations for their children that children cannot meet. This is particularly problematic for children who worry

or are fearful. Unconditional love remains an underlying principle for helping our children learn to deal with mistakes and perceived failure. It is when our children make mistakes and experience setbacks that our ability to be empathic is truly tested. Children can overcome much of their worry, fear, and anxiety if they are not burdened by the fear of mistakes and failures.

## Developing Responsibility, Compassion, and a Social Conscience

Young children are strongly motivated to be helpful, yet many parents tell us that their children have lost this drive by their middle childhood years. They appear to resist many opportunities to be of assistance unless there is something in it for them. In order for a pattern of helpful behavior to emerge and be maintained, parents must nurture this quality, shaping what may well be an inborn trait into a sense of responsibility, compassion, and social conscience. If parents take a narrow view of responsibility, suggesting that a child is irresponsible when a single task or chore is unfinished, and if their expectations are inconsistent with what their children can actually accomplish, their actions do little to help children develop responsibility. Following are four strategies to assist you in this important task:

1. *Serve as a model of responsibility.* As we have discussed before, when we act responsibly it increases the likelihood that our children will behave in a similar way.

2. *Provide opportunities for children to feel they are helping others.* Develop traditions to become a charitable family. A charitable family develops a tradition of involving the entire family in helping others. In doing so, you are reinforcing in your children the belief that they are important, they are capable of helping others, they are appreciated, and they can make a difference in their world.

3. *Responsibilities should be distributed evenly among family members.* It is important for everyone in the family to understand that they must each make a contribution.

4. *Take a helicopter view of your child's life.* A helicopter view helps to offset the narrow view we take sometimes by placing too much weight on one particular area and ignoring others. Taking a helicopter view will challenge you to observe your child's life from a broader perspective.

## Summary

We believe that a resilient mindset is essential for all children, but in particular for children who face greater adversity in their lives. Children who struggle with worry, fear, and anxiety experience such adversity, likely as the result of a combination of biological differences and experiences over time. For these children, developing a resilient mindset is critically important. Resilience conveys a sense of optimism, ownership, and personal control. Parents can serve as charismatic adults in the lives of their children, believing in them and providing them with opportunities that reinforce their islands of competence and feelings of self-worth.

# CONCLUSION

## Mastering Worry, Fear, and Anxiety

# Conclusion

# Mastering Worry, Fear, and Anxiety

In many ways, children today are fortunate to experience greater opportunities and technological advances than at any other time in history. Although it may be the best of times for children overall, unfortunate events worldwide, fueled by religious and political differences, have made this a very stressful and difficult time to be a child. In this environment, no child is immune to worry, and it would not be surprising for more children to develop fear and anxiety. If you have read this far in the workbook, it is our hope that you are feeling more optimistic and empowered to help your child. Put this empowerment into action. Though this may not always be an easy road, it is a road that is worth pursuing because learning to manage the stresses caused by worry, fear, and anxiety represents a significant insulating or protective factor as children transition into adult life. Learning to manage these problems is not a luxury, but rather a necessity for all children.

After reading this workbook, it is our hope that you have developed a better understanding of your role in helping children with worry, fear, and anxiety. You should now possess a good idea of the normal patterns of these problems, how they are defined, how to recognize them, and what to do.

Let's return to Bonneville Street. In the Gordon household, Michael and his parents have developed a plan to help him feel comfortable when he goes to bed at night. He has a nightlight in his room, a flashlight by his bedside, and a picture of his parents on his night table. He has decided to read before bed, choosing a number of favorite books to read as a means of helping him relax. Michael has also successfully had two sleepovers in the past month.

In the Barkley household next door, Susan has now attended school without an absence for the past four weeks. Susan has learned a number of stress-management strategies to help her worry less when she separates from her mother each morning. Although there have been some mornings when she has felt anxious and ill, Susan has agreed to go to school. Susan and her teacher have arranged a plan, such that, should Susan feel particularly anxious, she can leave the classroom for a period of time and go down to the nurse's office. Susan has only left the classroom once, returning within a half hour. Susan found visual imagery particularly helpful. When she feels anxious, she imagines herself at home with her parents and everything going well.

Down the street in the Gardner household, Kathy is beginning to overcome her fear of failure and her strong need for perfectionism at school. In addition to helping Kathy take tests with less stress, the Gardners consulted with the family physician who referred them to a child psychologist. The psychologist felt that Kathy's problems warranted structured counseling, and Kathy has been seeing a psychologist and has been learning different strategies to worry less and be more accepting of her performance.

Across the street, Marty has now been to the dentist. Marty and his mother made a number of trips to the dentist without Marty having to go in and have his teeth worked on. Marty chose a reinforcer that he would earn if he successfully visited the dentist. Finally, the dentist discussed with Marty a number of different interventions, including having Marty be asleep while the dentist worked on his teeth. Fortunately, Marty did not have any cavities and the dentist explained that all he would be doing is cleaning Marty's teeth. He showed Marty all of the tools, and together, they scheduled an appointment for the following week. Marty's teeth have now been cleaned. Through this process the Ellefsen family has discovered that Marty is fearful of a number of other things. Together, they have helped Marty feel comfortable in expressing his fears and have agreed to work with him whenever a fear provoking event arose.

Finally, in the Neilson household, despite the Neilson's efforts to help Lisa worry less, her worries progressed to the point where the family decided to seek help from their pediatrician. They were referred to a child psychiatrist who decided, along with the Neilsons, that a short-term trial of an anti-anxiety medication appeared warranted given Lisa's increasing problems. In the month since the medication has begun, Lisa is worrying significantly less. She can now openly talk about her worries. The family is scheduled to see a counselor to learn a number of additional strategies which they can use to help Lisa. The Neilsons have also helped their daughter recognize that sometimes worrying helps people plan ahead, as she demonstrated in bringing a plastic tarp along to a picnic, but that too much worry interferes with daily life.

We are confident and hopeful that *Seven Steps to Help Your Child Worry Less* will provide you with the guidance, assistance, and important information you need to be a consultant to your child and together develop helpful interventions. We hope this program will make a positive difference in your child's life and the life of your family. As always, we welcome your ideas and feedback. We wish you the very best with your children.

# Resources

**Resilience**

Brazelton, T.B. & Greenspan, Stanley I. (2000). <u>The Irreducible Needs of Children: What Every Child Must Have to Grow, Learn and Flourish.</u> Cambridge, MA: Perseus Publishing.

Goldstein, S. & Brooks, R. (2002). <u>Raising Resilient Children: A Nine Session Parenting Curriculum to Foster Strength, Hope and Resilience.</u> Baltimore, MD: Brookes Publishing.

Brooks, R. & Goldstein, S. (2001). <u>Raising Resilient Children.</u> New York, NY: Contemporary Books/McGraw-Hill.

Brooks, R. & Goldstein, S. (2002). <u>Nurturing Resilience in Our Children.</u> New York, NY: Contemporary Books/McGraw Hill.

Greenspan, S. & Lewis, N.B. (1999). <u>Building Healthy Minds: The Six Experiences that Create Intelligence and Emotional Growth in Babies and Young Children.</u> Cambridge, MA: Perseus Publishing.

Hallowell, E. (1996). <u>When You Worry About the Child You Love: Emotional and Learning Problems in Children.</u> New York, NY: Simon and Schuster Publishers.

Katz, M. (1997). <u>On Playing a Poor Hand Well - Insights from the Lives of Those Who have Overcome Childhood Risks and Adversities.</u> Chicago, IL: W.W. Norton and Company.

Levine, M.D. (1998). <u>Educational Care: A system for understanding and helping children with learning problems at home and in school.</u> Cambridge, MA: Educators Publishing Service.

Werner, E. & Smith, S. (1992). <u>Overcoming the Odds: High Risk Children from Birth to Adulthood.</u> Ithaca, NY: Cornell University Press.


**Attention Deficit Hyperactivity Disorder**
Barkley, R.A. (1995). <u>Taking Charge of ADHD: The Complete, Authoritative Guide for Parents.</u> New York, NY: Guilford Press.

Dendy, C.Z. (1995). <u>Teenagers with Attention Deficit.</u> Bethesda, MD: Woodbine House.

Goldstein, S. & Goldstein, M. (1992). <u>Hyperactivity: Why Won't My Child Pay Attention?</u> New York, NY: Wiley.

Hallowell, E.M. & Ratey, J.J. (1994). <u>Driven to Distraction.</u>   New York, NY: Pantheon Press.

Ingersoll, B. (1998).   <u>Daredevils and Daydreamers: New perspectives on ADHD.</u> New York, NY: Doubleday.

Jones, C. (1994). <u>ADD: Strategies for School Age Children.</u> San Antonio, TX:  Communication Skill Builders - A Division of Psychological Corporation.

Jones, C.B. (1991). <u>Sourcebook on Attention Disorders: A Management Guide for Early Childhood Professionals and Parents.</u> San Antonio, TX:  Communication Skill Builders - A Division of Psychological Corporation.

Parker, H.C. (1992). <u>The ADD Hyperactivity Handbook for Schools.</u> Plantation, FL: Specialty Press.

Rief, S.F. & Heimburge, J.A. (1998). <u>How to Reach and Teach All Students in the Inclusive Classroom: Read-to-Use Strategies, Lessons and Activities for Teaching Students with Diverse Learning Needs.</u> The Center for Applied Research in Education.

Rief, S.F. (1998). <u>The ADD/ADHD Checklist: An Easy Reference for Parents and Teachers.</u> New York, NY: Simon and Schuster Trade.

**Learning Disability and School Problems**
Brooks, R. (1991). <u>The Self-Esteem Teacher.</u> Loveland, OH: Treehaus Communications.

Goldstein, S. & Mather, N. (1998). <u>Overcoming Underachieving: An Action Guide to Helping Your Child Succeed in School.</u> New York, NY: Wiley.

Ingersoll, B. & Goldstein, S. (1993). <u>Attention Deficit Disorder and Learning Disabilities: Realities, Myths and Controversial Treatments.</u> New York, NY: Doubleday.

Levine, M. (1992). <u>All Kinds of Minds.</u> New York, NY: Educators Publishing Services.

Levine, M. (1996). <u>Keeping A Head in School.</u> New York, NY: Educators Publishing Services.

Mather, N. & Goldstein, S. (2001). <u>Learning Disabilities and Challenging Behaviors: A Guide to Intervention and Classroom Management.</u> Baltimore, MD: Brookes Publishing.

Strick, L. & Smith, C. (1999). <u>Learning Disabilities A to Z: A Parents' Complete Guide.</u> New York, NY: Simon and Schuster.

Zentall, S. & Goldstein, S. (1998). <u>Seven Steps to Homework Success: A Family Guide for Solving Common Homework Problems.</u> Plantation, FL: Specialty Press.

**Depression**

Ingersoll, B.D. & Goldstein, S. (2001). <u>Help for Your Unhappy Child: A Parent's Guide to Childhood Depression.</u> Plantation, FL: Specialty Press.

Clark, L. (1998). <u>SOS Help for Emotions: Managing Anxiety, Anger and Depression.</u> Bowling Green, KY: Parents Press.

**Anxiety**

Rapee, R.M., Spence, S., & Wignall, A. (2000). <u>Helping Your Anxious Child: A Step-by-Step Guide for Parents.</u> Champaigne, IL: New Harbinger.

Hallowell, E. (1998). <u>Worry: Hope and Help for a Common Condition.</u> New York, NY: Ballantine Books.

**Behavioral Problems**

Phelan, T.W. (1998). <u>1-2-3 Magic: Effective Discipline for Children 2-12</u> (2nd ed.). Glen Ellyn, IL: Child Management Press.

Phelan, T.W. (1998). <u>Surviving your Adolescents: How to Manage and Let Go of Your 13-18 Year Olds.</u> Glen Ellyn, IL: Child Management Press.

Clark, L. <u>SOS: Help for Parents.</u> Bowling Green, KY: Parents Press.

Greene, R.W. (1998). <u>The Explosive Child: A New Approach for Understanding and Parenting Easily Frustrated, Chronically Inflexible Children.</u> New York, NY: Harper Collins.

Barkley, R. (1998). <u>Your Defiant Child: Eight Steps to Better Behavior.</u> New York, NY: Guilford.

**Problem Solving**

Shure, M. (1994).  <u>Raising A Thinking Child.</u>  New York, NY: Henry Holt.

Shure, M. (2000).  <u>Raising a Thinking Preteen.</u>  New York, NY: Henry Holt.

**On-Line Resources**

Sam Goldstein, Ph.D. - "http://www.samgoldstein.com" <u>www.samgoldstein.com</u>
Articles and resources about childhood and adult conditions

Robert Brooks, Ph.D. - "http://www.drrobertbrooks.com" <u>www.drrobertbrooks.com</u>
Articles and resources about raising stress hardy children

Raising Resilient Children - "http://www.raisingresilientkids.com" <u>www.raisingresilientkids.com</u>
Learn more about resilience

ADD WareHouse- "http://www.addwarehouse.com"  <u>www.addwarehouse.com</u>
Articles, books, videos, assessment and trainng resources about ADHD across the lifespan and other related disorders

Children and Adults with Attention Disorders - "http://www.chadd.org" <u>www.chadd.org</u>
Articles and resources about ADHD across the lifespan

Learning Disabilities Association of America - "http://www.ldanatl.org" <u>www.ldanatl.org</u>
Articles and resources about learning disabilities across the lifespan

National Information Center for Children and Youth with Disabilities - "http://www.nichcy.org"
<u>www.nichcy.org</u>
Information on all disabilities and related issues

National Adult Literacy and Learning Disabilities Center - "http://novel.nifl.gov/nalldtop.htm"
<u>http://novel.nifl.gov/nalldtop.htm</u>
Publications, hot topics, links re LD and adult literacy

National Center for Learning Disabilities - "http://www.ncld.org" <u>www.ncld.org</u>
Information on all aspects of LD; resources, links

Anxiety Disorders Association of America - "http://www.adaa.org" <u>www.adaa.org</u>
Resources on various forms of anxiety conditions

Anxiety Panic Internet Resource - "http://www.algy.com" <u>www.algy.com/anxiety/index.shtml</u>
Resources on anxiety and panic disorders

National Institute of Mental Health - Anxiety Disorders - "http://panicdisorder.about.com/" http:/
/panicdisorder.about.com/
Treatment for anxiety disorders, including how to find the right professional help, resource guide

About.com - Panic and Anxiety Disorders - "http://panicdisorder.about.com/" http://
panicdisorder.about.com/
Panic disorder and its treatment, support groups, medication and stress management techniques

# Index

# SPECIAL ADDENDUM

## Special Addendum One
### A Guide for Medical and Mental Health Professionals
### Using the Seven Step Model as an Adjunct to Treatment

## Special Addendum Two
### Helping Children Worry Less:
### A Guide for Teachers

The following section was prepared as a guide for mental health professionals and teachers. These pages can be copied and provided to professionals interested in reviewing empirical research and practical guidelines about worry and anxiety in children.

# Special Addendum One

# A  Guide for Medical and Mental Health Professionals Using the Seven Step Model as an Adjunct to Treatment

From "Seven Steps to Help Your Child Worry Less" by S. Goldstein, K. Hagar and B. Brooks (Limited copies may be made for personal use.  Specialty Press, 2002)

---

In the past fifteen years, the number of books directed at helping parents deal with children who have a wide range of learning, mental health, behavioral, and medical problems has grown dramatically.  Today, it is rare when a mental health or medical professional consulted about a specific childhood problem does not recommend a book to assist parents in understanding their child's condition and in actively participating in an effective treatment process.  Even low incidence conditions, such as Autism, Obsessive/Compulsive Disorder and Tourette's Syndrome are covered by multiple volumes directed at parents.

But a quick visit to the local bookstore reveals an interesting phenomenon—the majority of the books on the shelves directed at helping parents, focus on externalizing conditions such as Attention Deficit Hyperactivity Disorder and Oppositional Defiance Disorder.  It is more difficult to locate books pertaining to the internalizing or non-disruptive disorders, such as anxiety, even though these may occur more frequently in the general population than in conditions related to externalizing behaviors.  There is no doubt that when a child is acting disruptively, parents are more likely to rush to the bookstore seeking assistance.

*Seven Steps to Help Your Child Worry Less* is meant as a guided manual for parents, but it is not a substitute for professional help in the diagnostic and treatment process.  In particular, children meeting the full symptom criteria for Generalized Anxiety Disorder, are likely to require assistance well beyond the parent-directed strategies offered in this manual.  However, it has also been well-documented across a variety of childhood conditions that parents are valuable, therapeutic agents.  This is particularly true to implement the cognitive behavioral strategies that have proven so effective in normalizing the overanxious behavior of affected children.

Although this manual focuses on children experiencing milder anxiety problems, we are convinced, based upon an emerging literature, that it can also serve as an important educational and therapeutic adjunct to a course of cognitive behavioral therapy for children experiencing a greater number of and/or severity of symptoms. This addendum will first provide an overview of current research concerning the conditions, subtypes, and definitions of worry, fear, and anxiety. This brief overview, which will include a description of the diagnostic process is not meant as a thorough review of the current literature nor as a complete guide to diagnosis. Interested readers are referred to March (1995). A framework for utilizing this program with families and their children on an individual basis in an outpatient clinic or school setting will also be reviewed.

## Background

Though anxiety disorders are common in children and teenagers and are frequently associated with impairment in all major life domains, much less is known about the internalizing disorders during these years than is known about disruptive problems, such as those related to Attention Deficit Hyperactivity Disorder, Oppositional Defiant Disorder, or Conduct Disorder. The co-morbidity rate of the internalizing disorders such as anxiety and depression is quite high with the externalizing disorders. Yet, in most clinical settings it is the disruptive, externalizing behaviors that are often the focus of assessment and treatment.

Worry, fear, and anxiety are terms that are often used interchangeably by the general public as well as many clinicians. However, in the seven step model, based upon current research literature, we have considered these three phenomena to fall along a continuum with worry reflecting the mildest problems followed by fear and finally, anxiety. Worry, fear, and anxiety are clearly different from a scientific basis. Worry reflects the inability to confidently predict a positive outcome for an upcoming event. It results from repeatedly thinking about the possible negative outcome for the prescribed event and being unable to substitute a more optimistic outlook.

For some individuals, worry may not be significantly impairing nor may it lead to fear. Fear, however, appears to be generated by worry and is best defined in physical terms. When fearful the body reacts aversively. When fear occurs individuals attempt to escape the fear-provoking event. Fear elicits a physiological response involving the sympathetic nervous system, including changes in heart rate, blood pressure, and hormones. A fear reaction may not necessarily be maladaptive. In fact, it is the physiological experience of fear that drives individuals to seek escape. Yet, at different ages, based upon a child's intellectual development, certain phenomena may invoke a fearful response simply based upon lack of knowledge. These types of developmental fears are outgrown by most children as they reach different maturational levels. The following table reflects common fears children experience at different ages (Klein, 1994).

| Fear | Age |
|------|-----|
| Loud noises, loss of support | Infancy |
| Strangers | 8 months |
| Separation from caregiver | 12-15 months |
| Fear of imaginary creatures | Early childhood |
| Fear about performance, health, and personal harm | Elementary age |

Further, the combination of worry and fear often leads to maladaptive behavior and ineffective problem solving. When these phenomena present repeatedly across multiple situations, causing impairment in everyday functioning beyond that which would be expected for most individuals, a diagnosis of anxiety is made.

The average child reports approximately eight stimulus-based worries spanning an average of six different categories. Most common worries relate to school, health, and personal harm. The number of worries a child possesses appears to correlate highly with their self-rating on the most commonly used anxiety scales (Silverman, La Greca, and Wasserstein, 1995). Interestingly, in samples of non-referred children, 30% report never worrying. Most children report worrying two to three times per week with the most common worries reflecting school, dying, becoming ill, or being teased. Females appear to worry more than males (Muris, Meesters, Merckelbach, Sermon, and Zwakhalen, 1998). Further, children with the highest self-reported anxiety demonstrate the weakest academic achievement. This raises an important question as to the source of anxiety. Are these children vulnerable to anxiety and thus their poor academic performance is the result of their emotional state? Is their emotional state the logical consequence of experiencing a learning disability? Or, for some children, could both phenomena be in effect? Teachers are often unaware of the extent to which some children experience anxiety (Ialongo, Edelsohn, Werthamer-Larsson, Crockett, and Kellam, 1994). Finally, multiple studies find the incidence of youth reported symptoms consistent with an anxiety disorder to range from 7% to 10%. When parents reports are utilized, anxiety disorders in children range from 4% to 16% (for review see Pliszka and Olvera, 1999).

As with most diagnostic systems for childhood conditions, the diagnostic system for anxiety problems in childhood continues to develop. For the moment, children and teens are expected to fit into the adult categories of anxiety, including Generalized Anxiety Disorder, Social or other Phobia, Panic Disorder, Post Traumatic Stress Disorder, or Obsessive/Compulsive Disorder. Only Separation Anxiety Disorder is considered a condition that emerges in the infancy, childhood or adolescent years, but not in adulthood.

It has also been found that children receiving diagnoses of anxiety disorders often receive more than one. For example, half of children with DSM III-R Overanxious Disorder were found to have Separation Anxiety Disorder as well in a study by Strauss and colleagues in 1988 (Strauss, Lease, Last, and Francis, 1988). In 1990, Benjamin and colleagues found that 25% of children with Separation Anxiety Disorder also experienced a Simple Phobia (Benjamin, Costello, and Warren, 1990). But the co-morbidity of anxiety disorders extends beyond just the borders of this category. In a number of studies, over a third of pre-adolescent children with Overanxious Disorder met the criteria for Attention Deficit Hyperactivity Disorder. Further, Strauss and colleagues found that 25% met criteria for Oppositional Defiant Disorder or Conduct Disorder (Strauss, et al., 1988).

It has also been well recognized that the sense of worry and apprehension that anxious children experience is often accompanied by feelings of helplessness or hopelessness. The more children worry and lack confidence in predicting an outcome, the more helpless and hopeless they feel about that outcome. Thus, in an escalating spiral, problems with worry appear to foster problems of helplessness and hopelessness, which often underlie the symptom presentation of depressive disorders. However, the overlap of depression and anxiety is uneven. Approximately a quarter of children with anxiety may meet a diagnosis for some type of depression. Yet, well over half and sometimes up to 75% of children with a depressive disorder will present combined anxiety (Angold and Costello, 1993). Thus, starting with feelings of helplessness and hopelessness may be more potent in leading children to worry than vice versa. Finally, a significant difference in co-morbidity for depression and anxiety is reported based upon age. In children under the age of eleven, less than 20% with Overanxious Disorder were found to meet criteria for depression. However, during the teen years, nearly half of those with an anxiety disorder were reported to experience co-occurring depression.

## The Diagnostic Process

Step two of this seven-step manual provides parents with a framework to determine when professional help is required. Thus, if parents arrive for assessment with this manual in hand, they have already considered certain thresholds and understand the severity of their child's problems. As noted, professional referral for problems related to worry, fear, and anxiety represents a small percentage of children referred to mental health clinics. For many children, what begins as a referral for disruptive behavior often leads to an understanding that multiple conditions, including anxiety are affecting a child's daily functioning. The diagnostic process for anxiety is similar to that for other childhood conditions. A careful, thorough history must be obtained. Clinicians must be aware of the normal developmental processes related to fears, the role the environment may play in fueling worry, and the diagnostic thresholds necessary to make a full syndrome Generalized Anxiety Disorder diagnosis. The age of onset of symptoms, the relationship of symptoms to life events, and the issues related to impairment must be well understood.

Further, in a clinic setting, it is often the rule rather than the exception that children with anxiety disorders will also demonstrate other disruptive and non-disruptive conditions.

Assessment should also include parent and teacher completed rating scales such as the Child Behavior Checklist (Achenbach & Edelbrock, 1991) or Conners Rating Scales (Conners, 1997). Depending upon the age of the child or teen, self-report measures such as the Revised Children's Manifest Anxiety Scale or Millon Adolescent Clinical Inventory should also be completed (see March, 1995; Pliszka and Olvera, 1999 for review of these procedures).

## Intervention

Although medications for the treatment of childhood conditions such as Attention Deficit Hyperactivity Disorder have become widely accepted in clinical practice, they continue to be controversial in the public eye. Unless a child experiences significantly impairing or debilitating anxiety, most medical or mental health professionals do not recommend medication intervention as an initial treatment of choice. In the future, as more research is completed, there may be medications which, along with parent and teacher training as well as cognitive behavioral therapy, help those children for whom anxiety represents a trait, learn to live their lives more effectively and with less stress. Readers interested in the current state of research concerning pharmacotherapy for anxiety problems are referred to March (1995). Although the anxiety medications in adults have been proven extremely effective, there are very few well-controlled studies of these agents in children and teens. The medicines studied have included tricyclic antidepressants, such as imipramine, and benzodiazepines and the selective serotonin re-uptake inhibitors, such as Prozac® and Zoloft®. The latter has proven effective in treating Obsessive/Compulsive Disorder and is now approved for children.

The seven-step model incorporates research-proven treatment plans and psychosocial treatments involving behavioral and cognitive interventions. The seven-step program is based on the tenets of cognitive behavioral therapy and Kendall's (1994) Cognitive Behavioral Therapy Approach. This form of cognitive behavioral intervention has been found effective on both individual and group bases (Beidel and Francis, 1995; Toren, Wolmer, Rosental, Eldar, Koren, et al., 2000). The seven-step model can be used with parents in a group treatment process. Therapists interested in a child or parent-child group for treating anxious children should also consider utilizing the *Coping Bear Workbook and Notebook* (Scapillato and Mendlowitz, 1994a and 1994b).

Therapists applying a cognitive behavioral approach to treating anxiety will find this workbook an excellent adjunct as a resource and support for parents. The desensitization model utilized in this text is based upon the work of Drobes and Strauss (1997). The model can be applied very efficiently to specific phobias as well as school refusal (Blagg and Yule, 1984). Techniques include modeling as well as contingency management. A variety of consequences can be used to extinguish unwanted behaviors while reinforcing a more appropriate response to worry, fear, and anxiety. The behavioral therapy component involves exposure to anxiety-provoking stimuli based upon the phobia treatment of Wolpe (1958).

# References

Achenbach, T.M. & Edelbrock, C. (1991). <u>Normative data for the child behavior checklist (rev.)</u>. Burlington,VT: Department of Psychiatry.

Angold, A. & Costello, E.J. (1993). Depressive comorbidityin children and adolescents: empirical, theoretical, and methodological issues. <u>American Journal of Psychiatry, 150,</u> 1779-1791.

Beidel, D. & Francis, G. (1995). Cognitive-behavioral psychotherapy. In: <u>Anxiety Disorders in children and Adolescents</u>. March JS, ed. New York: Guilford, pp 321-340.

Benjamin, R.S., Costello, E.J., & Warren, M. (1990). Anxiety disorders in a pediatric sample. <u>Journal of Anxiety Disorders, 4</u>, 293-316.

Blagg, N.R. & Yule, W. (1984). The behavioural treatment of school refusal: A comparative study. <u>Behavioral Research and Therapy, 22</u>, 119-127.

Conners, C.K. (1997). <u>Conners rating scales (Rev.)</u>. North Tonawanda, NY: Multi-Health Systems, Inc.

Drobes, D.J. & Strauss, C.C. (1997). Behavioral treatment of childhood anxiety disorders. <u>Child and Adolescent Psychaitric Clinics of North America, 6,</u> 779-793.

Ialongo, N., Edelsohn, G., Werthamer-Larsson, L., Crockett, L., & Kellam,S. (1994). The significance of self-reported anxious symptoms in first-grade children. <u>Journal of Abnormal Child Psychology, 22,</u> 441-455.

Kendall, P.C. (1994). Treating anxiety disorders in children: Results of a randomized clinical trial. <u>Journal of Consulting Clinical Psychology, 62,</u> 100-110.

Klein, R.G. (1994). Anxiety disorders. In M. Rutter, E. Taylor, & L. Hersov (Eds.). <u>Child and Adolescent Psychiatry: Modern approaches</u> (pp. 351-374). Oxford: Blackwell Scientific.

March, J. S. (1995). <u>Anxiety Disorders in Children and Adolescents.</u> New York, NY: Guilford Publishers.

Muris, P., Meesters, C., Merckelbach, H., Sermon, A., & Zwakhalen, S. (1998). Worry in normal children. <u>Journal of the American Academy of Child and Adolescent Psychiatry, 37,</u> 703-710.

Pliszka, S.R. & Olvera, R.L. (1999). Anxiety disorders. In S. Goldstein and C.R. Reynolds (Eds.). <u>Handbook of Neurodevelopmental and Genetic Disorders in Children.</u> New York, NY: Guilford Publishers.

Scapillato, D. & Mendlowitz, L. (1994a). <u>The Coping Bear Workbook.</u> Unpublished manuscript. Hospital for Sick Children. Montreal, Canada.

Scapillato, D. & Mendlowitz, L. (1994b). The Coping Bear Notebook. Unpublished manuscript. Hospital for Sick Children. Montreal, Canada.

Silverman, W.K., La Greca, A.M., & Wasserstein, S. (1995). What do children worry about? Worries and their relation to anxiety. Child Development, 66, 671-686.

Strauss, C.C., Lease, C.A., Last, C.G., & Francis, G. (1988). Overanxious disorder: An examination of developmental differences. Journal of Abnormal Child Psychology, 16, 433-443.

Toren, P., Wolmer, L., Rosental, B., Eldar, S., Koren, S., Lask, M., Weizman, R., & Laor, N. (2000). Case Series: Brief parent - child group therapy for childhood anxiety disorders using a manual-based cognitive-behavioral technique. Journal of the American Academy of Child and Adolescent Psychiatry, 39, 1309-1312.

Wolpe, J. (1958). Psychotherapy by reciprocal inhibition. Stanford, CA: Stanford University Press.

## Special Addendum Two

## Helping Children Worry Less:
## A Guide for Teachers

From "Seven Steps to Help Your Child Worry Less" by S. Goldstein, K. Hagar and R. Brooks
(Limited copies may be made for personal use.  Specialty Press, 2002)

---

# Introduction

Teachers are the experts when it comes to problems related to academic achievement. Parents, mental health professionals, and even physicians turn to teachers for guidance, advice, and instruction when children struggle academically. However, many teachers report being at a loss in knowing what to do when children demonstrate non-disruptive problems such as anxiety in the classroom.  First, it is often difficult to identify these problems because worrisome, fearful, or overanxious children are often indistinguishable in their general behavior from their classmates. Though problems related to school phobia are easy for teachers to observe and identify, the more common types of worry, fear, and anxiety that children experience are not.  Yet, during the school year, children, particularly in the elementary grades, typically spend more time with their classroom teacher than with other adults in their lives, often including their parents.

Even when teachers identify a child as a likely candidate for problems related to worry or anxiety, most are unsure or uncertain of how to proceed.  Physicians and parents often turn to teachers to help such children gain confidence and worry less.  Even mental health professionals whose primary responsibility it is to design and implement a program for children experiencing anxiety and excessive worry need teachers to understand these problems and serve as day-in and day-out real life supports and interventionists.  However, during their training, teachers are rarely exposed to education about worry and anxiety in children.  When they are provided with information, it is usually in a single class dealing with multiple childhood problems of which worry and anxiety may only be one. This brief guide will provide an overview of anxiety in children, discuss different types of anxiety and its presentation in the classroom, review causes of anxiety, explain the teacher's role in identifying and helping children with worry and anxiety, and finally, offer a set of classroom guidelines. This handout is not meant as a diagnostic tool. In fact, the teacher's primary role is not to diagnose, but to identify. In order to accurately identify children experiencing worry and anxiety, it is important that educators and administrators understand this condition and its warning signs.

# What is Worry?

Worry, fear, and anxiety are common human experiences. Interestingly, these terms are often used interchangeably despite the fact that they are distinct. Worry involves the rehearsal of possible aversive events to come and the apprehension that these coming events will not turn out well. Whether a test, playground activity, or homework assignment, worrisome children are often frozen with apprehension because of their inability to reassure themselves that they are competent and capable. Fear represents worry combined with a bodily alarm system preparing the child to face a real or perceived environmental threat. This bodily response, often referred to as "fight or flight," frequently involves multiple physical manifestations, the most common of which reflects children's complaints of aches and pains, particularly stomachaches. In the seven step model, worry often precedes the development of fear, and the two, over time, lead to anxiety. Anxiety represents a strong sense of apprehension or uneasiness. It is often related to a child's expectation that some kind of threat is present to his or her physical well-being. This sense of apprehension may be focused on an object, situation, or activity. For some children, however, this sense of anxiety appears to have a strong biological basis and is "free floating." Thus, it doesn't appear to be tied to a specific factor. These children are simply always on edge,

expecting the worst. Anxiety also has two other components: impairment, interfering with many activities of everyday life, and longevity. Thus, when a child is described as anxious, it is assumed that these are pervasive problems presented across many situations and experienced on a long-term basis without much relief.

In younger children, worry and fear often appear inseparable. As children grow older, these thoughts and fears change, varying in severity and occurrence. For example, some children demonstrate significant problems separating from their parents as they enter school as kindergarteners. This is the most common type of anxiety teachers observe. Despite repeated exposure to school, some of these children seem incapable of reassuring themselves that their family, parents in particular, will not be harmed nor will they move away forever during the brief separation of the school day. The stronger and lengthier children's experience of separation anxiety is, the more likely it is that they will experience other types of worry, fear, and anxiety as they grow older. Therefore, the earlier a child prone to anxiety and worry in the form of separation anxiety is identified and helped, the more likely these symptoms can be reduced and stressors related to these problems can be ameliorated in the future. In contrast, some children don't experience significant separation anxiety, but in response to a specific event they may develop an excessive fear. This type of fear is described as a phobia, in which the perceived fearful event is avoided at all costs.

Problems related to worry, fear, and anxiety are the most prevalent form of mental health difficulty across the life span. These problems come to the attention of the classroom educator when they impinge upon a child's classroom performance. Beyond problems separating and attending school, anxious children often struggle to relate effectively to others, complete school work, and, in many circumstances, are described as inattentive due to their quiet worry and rumination. The strategies used by anxious children to avoid school when school serves as a fear-provoking event (e.g., staying home) are based on a negative reinforcement model. What we mean by this is that the threat of school generates worry and fear. This hangs over the child's head, and the child attempts to avoid anxiety by avoiding school. School avoidance negatively reinforces the child and increases the likelihood that when he or she feels anxious tomorrow, the solution will be to avoid school. Though this can seem to the child to be an effective short-term solution, in the long run it only makes it more difficult for the child to conquer his or her fear of separation and dependence.

Symptoms of anxiety involve physical, behavioral, and cognitive or thinking components. Physical problems are often related to a system in the body known as the autonomic nervous system. This system is responsible for the regulation of internal bodily functions. Thus, symptoms of perspiration, stomachache, trembling, or even enuresis can be suggestive of anxiety. As noted, anxious children often complain of pain related to headache and stomachache.

In the thinking or cognitive realm, anxious children have difficulty freeing themselves of worrisome thoughts. They often draw erroneous conclusions about themselves, their capabilities, and the future. This then fuels worry and anxiety, which reinforces a sense of helplessness. Thus, it is not surprising that problems related to worry, fear, and anxiety frequently lead to unhappiness, and for some children, the additional problem of depression. Anxious children find it difficult to soothe themselves when worried.

They tend to distort potentially anxiety-provoking events, making a mountain out of a molehill.

On a behavioral basis, many anxious children do not come to the attention of teachers. As noted, anxiety is a non-disruptive problem in the classroom. Unlike problems related to disruptive behavior or Attention Deficit Hyperactivity Disorder, anxious children rarely disturb the flow of the classroom or act in ways that draw significant attention to themselves. Anxious children frequently worry in silence. An anxious fifth grader referred to the school psychologist for evaluation due to the teacher's concerns about problems with sustained attention, explained that during seat work he would begin looking around the room thinking the other students were doing their work better than he was. He then began to worry what the teacher would say or do if his work wasn't very good or was incomplete. Then he began to think about how his parents would respond, and suddenly he felt worried and unhappy that he wouldn't be able to play Nintendo. Just at that moment, his teacher asked him to please pay attention.

It is not until anxious children refuse school or break down emotionally that they come to the attention of their teachers as possibly experiencing problems related to anxiety. Anxious children often appear over-controlled in school and therefore rarely break the rules. As with our example, anxious children often come to the attention of teachers because of other real or perceived co-occurring problems such as Attention Deficit Hyperactivity Disorder. Behaviors such as fidgeting, being off task, or failing to complete work may often be interpreted as reflecting problems with attention. Some teachers mis-perceiving this problem respond punitively or with behavior management interventions which stand little chance of success. For some children, even well-intentioned actions by teachers often only serve to fuel the child's anxiety.

## Types of Worry, Fear, and Anxiety

Mental health professionals, including school psychologists, categorize childhood anxiety problems into a number of areas. These include Generalized Anxiety, Post Traumatic Stress Disorder, simple phobia, Obsessive/Compulsive Disorder, social phobia, and panic attacks. These problems are experienced by adults as well. The only diagnosis related to anxiety that is exclusive for children is that of Separation Anxiety. This diagnosis, as noted, often confronts teachers during the early elementary years.

*Separation Anxiety.* The essential feature of this problem is excessive worry about separation, usually from family members. Anxiety about separation from the mother is most commonly seen in young children. Separation anxiety is a typical developmental experience for children from approximately seven months of age to the early school years. In some children, separation anxiety appears to be experienced as a sense of panic. Other children appear to worry about potential dangers that threaten their family when they are separated. In response to separation anxiety, children often refuse to attend school, are reluctant to be alone, and frequently complain of physical symptoms.

Separation anxiety has been reported as the most common childhood problem. It is a problem that appears to occur more frequently in girls than in boys. Children between the ages of five and eight with this problem are likely to refuse to attend school. Older children frequently report distress at the time of separation from home. Teenagers with separation anxiety most commonly refuse to attend school and quickly develop a variety of physical complaints to justify

their behavior.

*Generalized Anxiety.* Children with Generalized Anxiety experience a sense of worry that is unfocused. This sense of apprehension appears to occur often for seemingly no defined reason. These children appear to be worry warts. They worry about future events, past behavior, and their competence. They often exhibit physical symptoms, are self-conscious, feel tense, find it difficult to relax, and require frequent reassurance. Their worries are often excessive and unrealistic.

In many situations, children with Generalized Anxiety are often aware that their discomfort is excessive. Girls experience Generalized Anxiety more commonly than boys. Intelligence or socio-economic status do not appear to be contributing factors. In extreme cases of generalized anxiety, some children also experience panic attacks. These feelings of panic can be precipitated by certain events. However, they most often occur for unexplained reasons. During such attacks, children often report feeling overwhelmed or drowning in a sea of physical symptoms that may include stomach pain, shortness of breath, dizziness, and a morbid apprehension that something terrible is about to happen. Children as young as three years can experience a panic attack, although the most common age at which this problem is identified in children is between the ages of eight and thirteen.

*Fears and Simple Phobias.* A simple phobia involves a specific, often isolated fear of a particular stimulus. Phobias are distinguished from fear of separation or panic attacks. They become problematic when the avoidant behavior interferes with normal functioning. Temporary fears are common in children. Many are age-specific or time- specific. Sometimes they originate with startled reactions to certain stimuli during the infancy or toddler years. More often than not, however, common fears such as those of bugs or snakes, do not emerge from a specific precipitating experience. Once again, girls report more fears and phobias than boys.

Children's fears change as they mature. Preschoolers are often fearful of animals and the dark. Sometimes difficulty distinguishing fantasy from reality may intensify fears in this age range. As children mature, realistic fears involving social and school issues often develop. By the teen years, fears most commonly reflect worry about competence in school and relationships with peers and family members.

Researchers have identified five distinct clusters of school-age children's fears. These include:
- fear of failure and criticism from adults
- fear of the unknown
- fear of injury in small animals
- fear of danger or death
- medical fear

When specific fears are evaluated, the ten most common fears identified in children are:
1. being hit by a car
2. not being able to breathe
3. a bombing attack
4. getting burned by a fire
5. falling from a high place
6. a burglar breaking into the home
7. earthquake
8. death
9. poor grades
10. snakes

Researchers have also found that children can reliably describe and rate the severity of their worry, fear, and anxiety. If you suspect that a child may be experiencing a specific fear, you should ask the child whether he or she is worried and then listen carefully to his or her con-

cerns. In the general population, a third of children report that they rarely worry, while the remainder report worrying two to three times per week, with the most common worries reflecting problems in school, dying, becoming ill, or being teased.

Serious phobias are generally unusual in children. In contrast, test anxiety is reported in nearly one-third of all students. At least one research study has reported a negative relationship between test anxiety and test performance. That is, the stronger a child's experience of test anxiety, the lower his or her test scores.

*Other Forms of Anxiety.* Obsessions are persistent, private thoughts or ideas, often of an unpleasant nature. They are intrusive and efforts to think about something else by the child often fail. Compulsions are repetitive, purposeful behaviors that often accompany obsessions. The purpose of these behaviors is to reduce the anxiety generated by obsessive thoughts. Sometimes these compulsions are described as rituals, such as repeated hand-washing or hair-combing. When these two sets of problems occur together with a fairly high level of intensity, they are referred to as Obsessive/Compulsive Disorder. This pattern of symptoms often causes children marked distress and is time consuming as rituals become longer and longer in duration in an effort to reduce anxiety. Although it is uncommon for teachers to observe severe obsessive/compulsive behaviors in children in the classroom, it has been increasingly recognized that children do, in fact, experience this condition in ways similar to adults. Children experiencing obsessive/compulsive problems often engage in lengthy preparatory behaviors involving arranging, checking, counting, and preparing for activities. Often these patterns of behavior become extensive and a child may consume most of his/her available work time just getting ready to work.

Post Traumatic Stress Disorder is a pattern of anxiety-related symptoms, including problems with concentration that result from experiencing, witnessing, or being confronted with an event or events involving actual or threatened serious injury or death. Children exposed to such events often respond with intense fear, helplessness, or horror. Symptoms of Post Traumatic Stress Disorder are somewhat distinct from other problems related to anxiety, including re-experiencing the event through intrusive thoughts or dreams, avoidance of settings, activities or stimuli associated with the trauma, difficulty sleeping, irritability and anger, disruption in school and social relations, and problems with mood and concentration. All children experiencing life-threatening events will demonstrate some of these symptoms. When they become impairing, a diagnosis is often made by a medical or mental health professional. When teachers are aware that a child has experienced such an event, the child should be closely monitored. Signs of significant disruption are reflected in the classroom by an abrupt change in behavior, relationships with others, and the quality of the child's schoolwork.

## Causes of Anxiety in Children

Nearly one in ten children is reported in research studies as experiencing problems with worry, fear, and anxiety to the point of impairment. Thus, in most classrooms, there will be two or three children experiencing these problems. These problems often reflect a basic, underlying temperamental risk or vulnerability. That is, on a biological or genetic basis, some children may be more prone to respond to life events with worry, fear, or anxiety. This biological risk may be general, and when interact-ing with a variety of environmental experiences, may lead some children to manifest excessive worry, fear, and anxiety. Children with Generalized Anxiety appear at the greatest risk to experience other problems, including phobias and panic attacks.

Given the genetic basis of this condition, it is not surprising that problems related to anxiety are more prevalent in some families than in others. The extent to which this reflects biology versus exposure to certain parental models, however, is not well-understood. Parents with anxiety problems are more likely to have children with anxiety problems. Even children described by their teachers as shy or behaviorally inhibited, but not necessarily experiencing severe difficulty, are more likely to have parents who, themselves, have histories of worry and anxiety.

## What Can Teacher Do

Worry, fear, and anxiety reflect a common underlying pattern of emotional distress. Because this distress rarely causes disruptive behavior in the classroom, particularly in the earliest stages, it is important for teachers to be well-educated and informed about the warning signs of these conditions. When you suspect that a child is struggling with these problems, you should discuss your concerns with the parents. With their input and permission, you can observe the child more carefully. Anecdotal notes, even a daily log completed over a one-week or two-week period, can be very helpful in identifying and defining the problem. Among the symptoms that may indicate a child is experiencing a problem with worry, fear, or anxiety are:

- passively off-task behavior
- a low emotional threshold
- resistance to participating in certain activities

- social isolation
- mild feelings of restlessness
- frequent complaints of illness involving stomachache or headache

Teachers are not responsible for labeling a child's behavior as caused by anxiety. Their role is to describe what they observe and then to organize that information to present to parents and school consultants. Teachers cannot and should not place themselves in a position of diagnosticians or therapists for that matter. Rather they should view themselves as important allies in helping students feel supported and accepted day after day. When working with children experiencing these problems, the teacher's role is to foster and implement strategies suggested by school consultants and work to make the classroom a place in which resilient qualities can thrive and the child can feel comfortable, accepted, and successful. Such qualities are reviewed in depth in step six of *Seven Steps to Help Your Child Worry Less* (Goldstein, Hagar and Brooks, 2002) as well as in the volumes *Raising Resilient Children* (Brooks and Goldstein, 2001, Contemporary Books/McGraw-Hill) and *The Self-Esteem Teacher* (Brooks, 1991, Treehaus Communications).

Teachers are not trained in the implementation of anxiety treatment interventions. However, basic awareness of these interventions and the role teachers play in them is valuable. Two types of treatments have been proven helpful for children experiencing worry, fear, and anxiety. These are behavior therapy and cognitive interventions.

Behavior therapy is the most effective intervention for children experiencing school refusal. Behavior therapy, also referred to as behavior modification, is based on the premise that specific behaviors are learned because they produce specific effects or consequences. Positive consequences, such as those that are pleasant or enjoyable, will strengthen behavior, making it more likely that the behavior will re-occur. Thus, when children are rewarded for appropriate behavior, it is likely they will exhibit the behavior again. Negative consequences or punishments are likely to reduce the behaviors that precede them. This is the basis for punishment when children misbehave. When children possess the ability to control their behavior but do not do so, punishment increases the likelihood they will make a better choice the next time. However, when children are unable to implement the better choice as the result of an interfering variable such as worry or fear, punishment is likely to be an ineffective intervention. As we discussed, children experiencing school refusal are often negatively reinforced over a long period of time, earning relief from their fear and anxiety by avoiding school.

Behavioral therapy approaches to the treatment of school refusal often contain multiple steps, including:

- reducing anxiety about school attendance through the use of systematic desensitization (approaching school in small steps);
- providing positive consequences for school attendance; and
- replacing positive consequences for school avoidance with negative consequences (eliminating the negative reinforcement model).

When a reward does not immediately follow a particular behavior, the behavior weakens slowly and eventually stops. Behavior is affected most powerfully by the consequences that immediately follow the behavior. Using principles of behavior modification, teachers can systematically arrange events so that positive consequences follow and thereby strengthen the appropriate, sometimes fear-confronting behaviors of children with anxiety. At the same time, undesirable behavior can be weakened and eliminated by ensuring that they are never followed by positive consequences or in some circumstances, following them quickly with negative consequences. Using this approach, teachers can intervene with a wide array of classroom problems. School psychologists can serve as consultants, helping teachers effectively analyze and set up successful intervention programs for the behavioral problems of anxious children in the classroom (Mather and Goldstein, 2001).

In contrast to behavioral interventions, cognitive interventions are focused on changing the way children think about themselves and the world around them. This form of intervention has been found to be extremely effective in improving the day in and day out functioning of children experiencing even severe anxiety problems such as those related to Obsessive/Compulsive Disorder. Teachers need to be aware, however, that simply engaging an anxious child in a logical discussion about their competence in the classroom and ability to complete work or tests successfully will not in a single trial dramatically alter the child's behavior. However, when this process is conducted over a long period of time in a supportive manner and accompanied with behavioral strategies, the combination has proven to be one of the most effective interventions for mental health problems.

## Eight Key Points to Helping Children with Worry, Fear, and Anxiety in the Classroom

1.  Remember that problems related to worry, fear, and anxiety are the most common across the age span. Worry, fear, and anxiety are real problems and are not the result of children not trying hard enough. To a milder degree, these problems are common for most individuals. Thus, they can be considered normal until they begin to cause significant daily impairment.

2.  Anxiety represents the extreme combination of worry and fear.

3.  Worry, fear, and anxiety are impairing in classroom performance but are not likely to be disruptive to the flow of the classroom. Thus, many children remain unidentified or incorrectly identified as experiencing other problems such as those related to Attention Deficit Hyperactivity Disorder or learning disabilities. Sometimes in response to these problems, however, children develop worry and anxiety.

4.  The classroom setting and the daily life of the child plays a key role in determining how children will experience and cope with worry, fear, and anxiety.

5.  Classrooms provide excellent environments to identify and help these children function more effectively.

6.  Teachers are important sources of emotional support for children with anxiety.

7.  The teacher's role is to identify and communicate, not diagnose or treat.

8.  Strategies to help children cope with worry, fear, and anxiety can be implemented effectively in the classroom. Often these strategies can be effective to help all children learn to cope with stress or adversity.

# References

Brooks, R. (1991). <u>The Self-Esteem Teacher.</u> Loveland, OH: Treehaus Communications.

Brooks, R. & Goldstein, S. (2001). <u>Raising Resilient Children.</u> New York, NY: Contemporary Books/McGraw-Hill.

Goldstein, S., Hagar, K., & Brooks, R. (2002). <u>Seven Steps to Help Your Child Worry Less: A Family Guide.</u> Plantation, FL: Specialty Press.

Mather, N. & Goldstein, S. (2001). <u>Learning Disabilities and Challenging Behaviors.</u> Baltimore, MD: Brookes Publishing.